**END**

MW01596418

Scott applies the gospel truths in a simple and understandable way to everyday problems we all face. I highly recommend this book if you desire to deepen your walk with Christ.

Sam Luke
Senior Pastor, Victory Tabernacle

Scott has written a practically relatable and spiritually encouraging book that will guide you step by step in a Biblical foundation as you grow in your Christian faith. His personal experiences and wisdom from God's Word can serve as a key to unlock the door to areas of advancement in your own life as well as increase for the Kingdom of God. This book is a joy to read while also being easy to apply because it is filled with grace and truth. I highly recommend adding this one to your library!

Joe Shutts
Senior Pastor, New Freedom Church
Author of **The Barnabas Principle**

Is it divine enablement? Or is it human responsibility? Or Both? Pastor Scott Fussnecker's insight is a must read for the serious seeker *"working out their salvation"* while knowing *"it is God who is working in you."*

Gary Keylan
Missions, Evangelism and Outreach Pastor, Redemption to the Nations Church

Way too often in my life I've tried to do the things only God could do, and I've put off or neglected the things He's patiently waiting on me to do. But if we're serious about following Christ, we must realize ... some of this is on US. Thankfully, in the following pages, my friend Pastor Scott Fussnecker provides timely and game-changing wisdom, straight from God's Word and from his own life. I hope you'll read this book today and then buy a few copies for your friends.

Tony Byrd
Senior Pastor, MorningStar Church

Pastor Scott Fussnecker comes from a great line of godly men and women. He carries a generational blessing, as being part of a ripple effect, not just the splash. I am sure you will be strengthened, equipped, and encouraged as you read through the pages of this book. God has given Scott a fresh revelation on perseverance. Read this book and let this book read you.

Matt Morgan
Senior Pastor, Fellowship of Praise
Author of **Supernatural Power on Earth**

ACTIVATING THE POWER OF GOD IN YOUR LIFE

THAT'S ON YOU!

SCOTTFUSSNECKER

THAT'S ON YOU! Activating the Power of God in Your Life
Published by Scott Fussnecker
100 Sal Blvd
Trenton OH 45067
scott@foundationcincy.com

Unless otherwise noted, all scripture quotations are taken from the Holy Bible, New International Version®, NIV® Copyright © 1973, 1978, 1984, 2011 by Biblica, Inc.® Used by permission of Zondervan. Accessed online at Biblehub.com. All rights reserved worldwide. www.zondervan.com

Scripture quotations marked (AMP) are taken from The Amplified Bible. Copyright © 2015 by The Lockman Foundation. Accessed online at Biblehub.com. All rights reserved www.lockman.org.

Scripture quotations marked (KJV) are taken from King James Version, public domain and may be quoted freely without attribution. Accessed online at Biblehub.com.

Scripture quotations marked (TPT) are taken from The Passion Translation® is a registered trademark of Passion & Fire Ministries, Inc. Copyright © 2020 Passion & Fire Ministries, Inc. All rights reserved. ThePassionTranslation.com

Scripture quotations marked (NLT) are taken from *Holy Bible, New Living Translation,* copyright © 1996, 2004, 2015 by Tyndale House Foundation. Used by permission of Tyndale House Publishers, Inc. All rights reserved.

Biblical word studies are taken from *Strong's Expanded Exhaustive Concordance* (James Strong. Thomas Nelson Publishers, 2009), *HELPS Word Studies* © (Helps Ministries, Inc.1987, 2011) and *Strong's Greek Lexicon* ©. *Thayer's Greek Lexicon,* Electronic Database. © 2002, 2003, 2006, 2011 by Biblesoft, Inc. All rights reserved. Used by permission. BibleSoft.com

Digital quotations taken from BibleHub.com, accessed online Dec. 2024–Mar. 2025. Bible Hub is a production of the Online Parallel Bible Project.

TABLE OF CONTENTS

DEDICATION

This book is dedicated to my late Father-in-Law, Dr. Jim McPherson, whose commitment to the study of God's Word inspired countless hearts and minds. His life is a testament to the power of wisdom and devotion to the Lord. May his legacy continue to lead others in the pursuit of truth and understanding.

ACKNOWLEDGEMENTS

First and foremost, I must acknowledge the power of God's divine revelation, which has guided me in putting these words to paper. God is the true foundation of this work.

A special thank you to my day one support system—my beautiful wife, Jennifer. Your love, patience, and belief in me have been my strength throughout this entire process. To my kids and their families, who are my world, thank you for filling my life with joy, purpose, and meaning.

To my mom and dad, who will proudly tell anyone this book is great, whether they actually believe it or not (lol)—your love and encouragement have been the pillars of my life. You always made me believe that I could do anything I set my mind to. I didn't realize the value of that until I grew a little older. Thank you for being the godly examples that you are. You'll never truly know what you mean to me!

To my sister Kim, I don't say it much, but you have impacted me more than you realize. To my brother Russ, you have paved an amazing pathway for me to follow in my career and ministry.

Thank you to my mother-in-law Kaye McPherson. Your influence, along with Jim's, are stamped all over this book.

Thank you to my editor, Carol Smith, who has probably forgotten more about the Bible than I could ever hope to know. Your expertise, insight, and challenging questions pushed me to refine my thoughts and make this work better than it ever could have been on my own. I'm truly grateful for your guidance, Carol.

Thank you to my friend and graphic designer Brian Suman. Your talent and creativity are off the charts. When I was thinking of who could help with the design of this book, you were the first person I called. You said "Scott, I have never designed a book cover." I replied,

"I don't care Brian, you're still the best." Lol! The best make everything look easy.

Finally, I want to say thank you to the Foundation Family. You all treat me better than I deserve. Your love and support have made a lasting impact on my life.

Through all the challenges and victories, writing this book has reinforced what I've always believed: We truly are "better together."

INTRODUCTION

I'm writing this book with a desire to bring believers to full awareness of how to activate the power of God in their lives. As a pastor, I long to see God's people experience His sustaining, overcoming power, thriving, and healthy in every way. For many years, I've seen people start a relationship with God with zeal and enthusiasm, only to see them eventually fizzle out. Many times, they fizzle out to the point that they no longer have the same desire to please God that they once did. I mean, they used to volunteer at church, financially support the Kingdom, have a strong prayer life, and a godly impact on those around them.

Sometimes I call these people "your first in, last out." (Side note: If you happen to be in a leadership position reading this book, never forget "your first in, last out" people.) These are the people who unlock the door, turn off the alarm, set the thermostats, start the coffee, and make sure things are ready for the day. Then at the end of the day, they clean out the coffee, reset the thermostats, turn on the alarm, and lock the doors. Somehow and some way, these same people burn out and fizzle out—then, you only see them attend church once in a month of Sundays. Not that attending church, acts of service, or financial giving makes you a Christian, but these things are usually a manifestation of a deeper relationship with God and a desire to please Him.

On the other hand, I have seen many people give their heart to God, and their lives are radically and completely changed. The trajectory of their life begins to change for the better, and they never look back. All the sudden, their future has hope attached to it. Jeremiah 29:11 (NIV) says, *"For I know the plans I have for you," declares the Lord, "plans to prosper you and not to harm you, plans to give you hope and a future."*

So, what is behind all of this? What really makes the difference between one person experiencing and sustaining the mighty power of God in their life and another person who seems to never gain any spiritual traction or one who fizzles out? It's the same God, but different outcomes in life. Does God show favoritism? The answer to that is simple: God does not show favoritism! God is no respecter of people. God sent His Son to die for ALL. It is God's desire that all people come to the saving knowledge of Jesus Christ and give their hearts to him, then experience a full and abundant life.

THE BIBLE CAN BE DESCRIBED AS TWO PARTS: "THE PERSON OF GOD AND THE PRINCIPLES OF GOD." IT'S IMPORTANT NOT TO GLOSS OVER OUR RESPONSIBILITY TO LIVE OUT THE PRINCIPLES OF GOD IN LIFE!

A friend of mine, Richie Mullis who Pastors at FreeLife Church in Texas, once said, "God is no respecter of persons; however, He is a respecter of principles." Those words stuck with me as a divine revelation of the importance of living out the principles of God in your life. Over the years, I've heard the Bible described in two parts: "the person of God and the principles of God." It's important not to gloss over our responsibility to live out the principles of God in life! It is not automatic. This is the part *that's on you*—your responsibility.

Let me try to explain: As a young boy growing up in a full-Gospel Pentecostal church, I had become very keen to the Spirit of God. From a very young age, I knew that God had given me the free will to influence the spiritual outcomes in my life. Notice I used the word "outcomes," and not "consequences." Sometimes I've made good spiritual decisions in my life that have produced positive outcomes and Christian progress, albeit slow progress at times. However, there have been other times in my life that I've made poor spiritual decisions and as a result, I experienced setbacks in life that have been very difficult to overcome. By the grace and mercy of God, I kept getting back up to take another step toward God.

After many years of a cyclical pattern of living like this, I received a word from God that was clear and simple. He said, "Scott, THAT'S ON YOU." As I recall, I received this word from God when I was around 19 years old. As I prayed and reflected on the condition of my life at that time, I realized that something in me had to change. I knew that God's grace and mercy had me covered, but I was beginning to realize that God's grace and mercy aren't free passes to do whatever you want. I began to realize that the decisions I was making outside of the will of God for my life were setting the course of my life back a great deal.

I'm not sure I learned enough about that in the churches I grew up in. Not that the churches I grew up in were bad; in fact, most of the experience was good. Many churches like the ones I grew up in tend to teach, "Just turn it over to God and He will make it right" or "Name it and claim it." I agree, sometimes that is all that it takes; turn it over to God and He will make it right. Nevertheless, in time, I've also learned that God is not a magic wand that you can simply wave and all the sudden life is easy. I always tell my congregation at Foundation Community Church (Foundation) that life is hard, the devil is real, but God is good.

The church at-large often preaches the message that all you must do is give your heart to God and He will change your life for the better; it's that easy! Well, yes and no. Now, before you close this book and accuse me of preaching false doctrine, let me explain. The message that giving your heart to God will change your life for the better is true. The rest of the story is to be written along the way with God, as you pursue practical sanctification. The process of practical sanctification is multifaceted and can be painfully agonizing sometimes.

I just threw a big religious word at you, "sanctification." So churchy sounding! But what does it mean? It means "the action or process of being freed from sin or purified." Sounds simple, but that's deeper than you may think!

This book is about equipping you to live your life according to the plan and purpose that God has for you. To that end, questions and thoughts to help you walk that out are provided at the end of each Principle Scripture. These points are called "Applying This Principle—That's on You!"

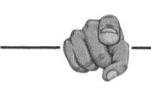

BUT THE ONE WHO DOES NOT KNOW AND DOES THINGS DESERVING OF PUNISHMENT WILL BE BEATEN WITH FEW BLOWS. FROM EVERYONE WHO HAS BEEN GIVEN MUCH, MUCH WILL BE DEMANDED; AND FROM THE ONE WHO HAS BEEN ENTRUSTED WITH MUCH, MUCH MORE WILL BE ASKED.

- LUKE 12:48

They can be used for personal devotion or for group study, and will help you put a finger on areas that you may need to reevaluate in order to live by these principles. Be honest with yourself, so that you can apply them, fully activate God's power in you, and see Him go to work on your behalf!

Much of living out God's plan for your life hinges upon your obedience to the Word of God; that's where sanctification comes in. Living out purpose is *not* just all on God! In fact, the "living it out" part—THAT'S ON YOU! Throughout this book I'm going to illuminate scriptures from God's word that require much of born-again believers (Luke 12:48). Henceforth the term, *THAT'S ON YOU!*

PART ONE:
COMING TO KNOW THE PERSON OF GOD

THAT'S ON YOU!

PART ONE:
COMING TO KNOW THE PERSON OF GOD

The Person of God

Before getting into more specific principles of God that we should live by, I think it's important to talk about the person of God. This will help us know Him better, so we can fully trust Him to perform the part of the covenant that's on Him.

God exists in three persons: God the Father, God the Son, and God the Holy Spirit. God existed before anything existed. Genesis 1:1-2 tells us, *"In the beginning God created the heavens and the earth. Now the earth was formless and empty, darkness was over the surface of the deep, and the Spirit of God was hovering over the waters."*

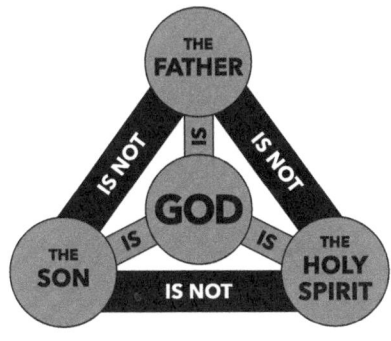

In what the Bible describes as 6 days, the person of God spoke into existence the heavens and the earth. As we read this verse from Genesis, we can easily see the evidence of God the Father and God in Spirit. While not immediately evident, Jesus was also present at Creation, as the manifest Word God spoke, bringing all things into being. We read later in Scripture about God manifesting Himself in the physical body, as the third part of the Godhead, known as the Son of God, or Jesus. However, Jesus was also eternally existent and in union with the Trinity from before the Creation of all things, as we see in the following verses:

In the beginning was the Word, and the Word was with God, and the Word was God. He was in the beginning with God. All things were made through Him, and without Him nothing was made that was made. (John 1:1-3)

THE SAME GOD WHO SPOKE LIGHT INTO THE CHAOTIC DARKNESS AT CREATION STILL SPEAKS LIGHT AND BRINGS ORDER INTO THE CHAOS OF OUR LIVES.

The same God who spoke light into the chaotic darkness at Creation still speaks light and brings order into the chaos of our lives. The same Holy Spirit hovers over people today to draw them to Jesus, the Word of God, so that He can be made manifest in our bodies of earthen clay. He will transform our lives by the power of His glory within us. As Paul said in 2 Cor. 4:6-7, *"For God, who said, 'Let light shine out of darkness,' made his light shine in our hearts to give us the light of the knowledge of God's glory displayed in the face of Christ. But we have this treasure in jars of clay to show that this all-surpassing power is from God and not from us."*

Before going any further, I feel like this would be a good place to provide you with some encouragement and confidence that you can trust God to fulfill His side of the covenant you make when you come into relationship with Him. Jesus is trustworthy—said another way, God is worthy of our trust. And, when you trust Him, blessings follow:

For the LORD God is a sun and shield; the LORD bestows favor and honor; no good thing does he withhold from those whose walk is blameless. LORD Almighty, blessed is the one who trusts in you. (Psalm 84:11-12)

He's never failed and He won't start now. He's never lied and He cannot. If He were to speak a lie, it would immediately be created as truth—that's the power in His words, the same Voice that spoke Creation into existence and upholds it to this day.

Because God wanted to make the unchanging nature of his purpose very clear...in which it is impossible for God to lie, we who have fled to take hold of the hope set before us may be greatly encouraged. We have this hope as an anchor for the soul, firm and secure. (Hebrews 6:17-19a)

Be encouraged! Anchor your soul in the fact that He cannot lie and will bless you as you **trust** in Him—*THAT'S ON YOU!* He will fulfill His side of the covenant and, as you will see, will enable you to keep your side as well—*THAT'S ON HIM!*

He's Promised to Redeem Your Past

Sometimes, we feel like we've sinned too big or too much for God to work in our lives. Let me remind you of what the Apostle Paul tells us in Romans 3:23, *"For ALL have sinned and fall short of the glory of God."*

Well then, that's a relief! I hope you can see that you are not alone! Paul continues with this theme of people and sin in Romans 5:12: *"Therefore, just as sin entered the world through one man, and death through sin, and in this way, death came to ALL people, because ALL sinned."*

In these verses, ALL means ALL. There are no exemptions or free passes. If you are reading this, you have sinned, and by the grace and mercy of God, you can be forgiven. Don't believe the lie of the enemy that says your past is what defines you, it's just too much to overcome. In almost 30 years of ministry, I've watched God use people that have a past that would blow you away. Stories of addiction, abuse, deception, lapse in judgement—you name it and I've probably heard it or seen it!

Fortunately, the Bible tells us *"We know that in ALL things God works for the good of those who love Him, who have been called according to His purpose"* (Romans 8:28). Again, ALL means ALL. So,

THE NEXT TIME THE ENEMY STARTS TO WHISPER IN YOUR EAR THAT YOUR PAST IS WHAT DEFINES YOU, REMEMBER:

YOU ARE WHO GOD SAYS YOU ARE.

the next time the enemy starts to whisper in your ear that your past is what defines you, remember: *You are who God says you are.* You are not defined by the world, you are not defined by the lies of the enemy, and you are not defined by your past. In fact, God takes even the most checkered pasts and turns them into testimonies and stories of His redemption. Praise God for redemption!

God Desires Relationship

Let's go just a bit deeper here to make this clear to understand. Sin and disobedience entered the world when Adam and Eve disobeyed God in the Garden of Eden. They sinned because they were deceived by the enemy. In time, God spoke to Moses in the Old Testament and brought the written Law into the world by way of the Ten Commandments. This was called the Mosaic Covenant, or the Covenant of Law. These commands were non-negotiable instructions for the children of God to live by in order to please God. Spoiler alert: The Israelites were not very good at obeying these commands. Even with a written law and the spiritual leadership that they had in Moses, they couldn't (or wouldn't) overcome their sin and disobedience.

For hundreds of years the children of God attempted countless ways to bring themselves back into right relationship with Him through a system of sacrifices. They just couldn't seem to overcome the disease of sin inherited from our first parents, Adam and Eve. From that original sin in the Garden and throughout the Old Testament, the children of God would sacrifice, then sin, repeatedly.

Pro Tip: You can't work or sacrifice yourself into a right relationship with God. Try as we might, we cannot live a life pleasing to God in our own strength. The only way to do it is by Him working through us by the power of His own Spirit within us. This is why we need to activate His power in our own lives.

So, God provided a way to reconcile us back to Himself. God's plan of salvation to bring us back to Him came by way of sending His Son, Jesus, to save the world. John 3:16 tells us that *"God so loved the world that he gave his one and only Son, that whoever believes in him shall not perish but have eternal life."*

THE ONLY WAY TO DO IT IS BY HIM WORKING THROUGH US, AND BY THE POWER OF HIS OWN SPIRIT WITHIN US. THIS IS WHY WE NEED TO ACTIVATE HIS POWER IN OUR OWN LIVES.

God's Power Makes Us Covenant-Keepers

When you accept Jesus as Savior, you are making a covenant with God. Bible Dictionaries define it this way:

A covenant, in biblical terms, is a solemn agreement or promise between God and humans, or between human parties, that establishes a relationship with specific commitments and obligations....Covenants in the Bible reveal God's desire to enter into a relationship with humanity, characterized by promises and obligations.... Where one of the parties is infinitely superior to the other, as in a covenant between God and man, there God's covenant assumes the nature of a promise, Isaiah 59:21 Jeremiah 31:33,34 Galatians 3:15-18. (Biblehub.com accessed online 2.5.25)

Notice that a covenant is an agreement with specific commitments required of each party. When you form this covenant with God, you can be assured that *God will fulfill His side* of the covenantal relationship. However, *you will fail* at fulfilling your side of the covenant. Right

GOD SAW THAT THE PEOPLE OF ISRAEL DIDN'T KEEP THE LAW, AND TRUTH BE TOLD, NO ONE CAN. THIS IS WHY JESUS MADE THE COVENANT HIMSELF ON OUR BEHALF, AND HE NEVER FAILS TO KEEP HIS OATHS!

now, you may be thinking, "Wait, what? I thought having a relationship with God would make life easy and everything would be good."

God knows that humanity is incapable of complete obedience because we have free will. He's given us the privilege of making our own choices and deciding whether or not to love and follow Him. He saw that the people of Israel didn't keep the Law, and truth be told, *no one can*. This is why He decided to replace the Law, or Mosaic Covenant, with the New Covenant so that it couldn't fail. This is *why Jesus made the covenant Himself on our behalf*, and He never fails to keep His oaths!

But God found fault with the people and said:

"The days are coming" declares the Lord, "when I will make a new covenant with the people of Israel and with the people of Judah. It will not be like the covenant I made with their ancestors when I took them by the hand to lead them out of Egypt, because they did not remain faithful to my covenant, and I turned away from them," declares the Lord.

*"This is the covenant I will establish with the people of Israel after that time," declares the Lord. "**I will put my laws in their minds and write them on their hearts**. I will be their God, and they will be my people.... For I will forgive their wickedness and will remember their sins no more."*

By calling this covenant "new," he has made the first one obsolete; and what is obsolete and outdated will soon disappear. (Hebrews 8:8-12)

Jesus was both our covenantal sacrifice and representative when this New Covenant was made. By His Holy Spirit, He has written His laws and principles on our hearts and minds rather than on stone tablets. By His Spirit within you, you have a new nature and character. And by the power of that Spirit, you have the ability to fulfill His desires because He's made them your own by writing them within you!

BY THE POWER OF HIS SPIRIT, YOU HAVE THE ABILITY TO FULFILL HIS DESIRES. HE'S MADE THEM YOUR OWN BY WRITING THEM ON THE TABLETS OF YOUR HEART.

Giving your heart to God assures you of the promise that you will have eternal life. However, it doesn't mean you will no longer tempted by the enemy. The same enemy that tempted and deceived Adam and Eve, will tempt and try to deceive *you*. The good news of Jesus is that surrendering your life to God means you can be forgiven because of the grace of God, even when you have given in to temptation.

This salvation that you receive will draw you to strengthen your faith and develop an even deeper relationship with God. In fact, grace "primarily refers to the unmerited favor and kindness of God towards humanity. It [also] encompasses the idea of divine assistance given to humans for their regeneration and sanctification" (*Strong's*). We see here the word "grace" carries with it a meaning of empowerment, or divine enablement.

The Greek word translated "grace" in the New Testament is *charis*, and this is where we get the words charity, charisma, and charismata (spiritual power gifts). A charismatic person possesses a grace and power that flows from them and attracts, encourages, and blesses others. *Thayer's Lexicon* includes the meanings, "the spiritual condition of one governed by the power of divine grace...capacity and ability due to the grace of God."

WHEN YOU COVENANT WITH GOD, YOU RECEIVE A NEW NATURE GOVERNED BY THE POWER OF DIVINE GRACE. YOUR NEW SPIRIT HAS SUPERNATURAL CAPACITY AND ABILITY DUE TO THE GRACE OF GOD.

When you come into covenant with God, His grace draws you to love Him and empowers you to love and help others as well. His power enables you to keep covenant and win the race set before you. I love what Hebrews 12:1-3 say about this: *"Let us also lay aside every weight, and sin which clings so closely, and let us run with endurance the race that is set before us, looking to Jesus, the founder and perfecter of our faith"*

Make Your Covenant with God

My prayer is that through the principles taught in this book you will better understand just how faithful God is, and that truth will compel you to strengthen your side of your relationship with God. He is faithful and true to fulfill His side of the relationship. The sins you've committed in the past don't matter; your failures don't matter; your shortcomings don't matter. This is why God sent His Son to be the sacrifice for your sins; because you alone can't overcome your sins, but you can be forgiven.

This is a good time to offer you an opportunity for salvation. Maybe you haven't begun a relationship with God and you want to. The first step in beginning a relationship with God is to acknowledge and turn from sin (repentance). Confess your sin to Him and ask for forgiveness on the basis of Christ's death. Relinquish control of your life to Him, making Him Lord. This is what the Bible calls being born again.

Talk to Him as your own Father, in your own words, and make space for Him to talk to you about your life and His plans for you. Pray a prayer something like this: "God forgive me of my sins, come into my heart. I believe that you sent your Son, Jesus, to die for me."

If you just said this prayer for the first time and you believe it in your heart, you are born again. You are now a son (or daughter) of God and have begun a relationship with Him as your Father. After being born again, you have a new life to live on this earth, a life free from sin and the nature of fallen man. You just formed a spiritual covenant with God! If I were texting you right now, this is where I would put several emojis like praise hands, fist bumps, checkmarks, or prayer hands.

AFTER BEING BORN AGAIN, YOU HAVE A NEW LIFE TO LIVE ON THIS EARTH, A LIFE FREE FROM SIN AND THE NATURE OF FALLEN MAN.

EXPERIENCING THE POWER OF GOD

THAT'S ON YOU!

PART TWO:
EXPERIENCING THE POWER OF GOD

The All-Encompassing Power of God

God is all-powerful and has attributes belonging only to Him by virtue of His triune being, the Father, Son, and Holy Spirit. This power is sometimes called divine, or supernatural power; in other words, power that can only come from God. The three facets of the power of God are referred to as omnipotence, omniscience, and omnipresence. The prefix "omni" means "all or everywhere." Only God can have the attribute of "all or everywhere." When you add the word "potent," which means to have power, you of course get omnipotent. To be omnipotent is to be all-powerful. When you add the word "science," you get omniscience, meaning all-knowing. Finally, when you add the word "presence," you get omnipresence, meaning God is always everywhere.

Seems impossible to wrap a finite human mind around sometimes, but that's because these are divine attributes, not human attributes. In many ways, these three descriptors help us understand just how powerful God really is. It's His power you need to activate in order to receive all that God has for you. How amazing that He wants to share His power with us!

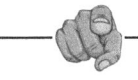

IT'S HIS POWER YOU NEED TO ACTIVATE IN ORDER TO RECEIVE ALL THAT GOD HAS FOR YOU. HOW AMAZING THAT HE WANTS TO SHARE HIS POWER WITH US!

God's Power Activated in Us!

I want to take a moment to explain to you how this happens. It may take a little time but it's important to know and understand. If you desire to activate the power of God in you, listen up!

As we've seen, His grace, or divine enablement, comes into us when we make covenant with Him; we are born again of the Holy Spirit and made a son or daughter of God.

> *But as many as received him, to them gave he power to become the sons of God, even to them that believe on his name: Which were born, not of blood, nor of the will of the flesh, nor of the will of man, but of God. (John 1:12-13 KJV)*

Being born of God is a work of the Holy Spirit; His indwelling presence is within us, leading, guiding, teaching, *yet there is much more!* Our Father wants to bring us into full, mature sonship, so that we do the works that Jesus did. He came to Earth as a man to show us how to live as His image bearers, just as He had originally intended for Adam and Eve. He became the Son of Man so that we could become sons of God.

We'd all have to admit that we often don't manifest the power of the Son of God, as He instructed His disciples:

> *Very truly I tell you, whoever believes in me will do the works I have been doing, and they will do even greater things than these, because I am going to the Father. (John 14:12)*

What's missing in our own experience and in many churches? It's the power of the Holy Spirit flowing through His sons and daughters!

Jesus, Our Pattern for Power

Jesus performed many miracles by the Spirit of God within Him, modeling the activation of God's power in a type of pattern. He laid aside His glory (Phil. 2:5-8) and put on a body of flesh (John 1:14); Jesus was both fully God and fully man. As a Son of man, He experienced the grief and pain of humanity (Isaiah 53:2-6; John 11:33-36; Luke 9:41). Just as we are, Jesus was born of the Spirit (Luke 1:26-28). As He instructed us to do, He was water-baptized at the Jordan River, and the Holy Spirit came to rest upon Him. The Dove didn't depart because Jesus walked in a way so as not to grieve the Spirit (Matt. 3:13-16). It was after this that the Holy Spirit led Him to the desert for a period of fasting and consecration, so that He was empowered when He came back among the people. It was only then that His miraculous ministry began (Matt. 4:1-17).

JESUS WAS EMPOWERED AFTER A PERIOD OF FASTING AND CONSECRATION. AFTER THIS, HE CAME BACK AMONG THE PEOPLE AND HIS MIRACULOUS MINISTRY BEGAN.

This is the pattern for us; this is why I earlier said we need "practical sanctification," to be consecrated and baptized with power as the Holy Spirit comes upon us. This is what John the Baptist foretold when he baptized Jesus at the Jordan:

> "I baptize you with water for repentance. But after me comes one who is more powerful than I, whose sandals I am not worthy to carry. He will baptize you with the Holy Spirit and fire." (Matthew 3:11)

Before His Ascension, Jesus affirmed John's words:

> On one occasion, while he was eating with them, he gave them this command: "Do not leave Jerusalem, but wait for the gift my father promised, which you have heard me speak about. For John baptized with water, but in a few days, you will be baptized with the Holy Spirit." (Acts 1:4-5)

If I were preaching right now, I would be beside myself. Sometimes my Pentecostal roots get the best of me, and I want to shout! Can I get an Amen!?

Power Will Come Upon You!

If you want the power of God to be activated in your life, you must catch this next verse: *"But you will receive power when the Holy Spirit comes upon you"* (Acts 1:8). Did you catch that? You receive power *when the Holy Spirit comes upon you!* Many believe that a prayer of salvation and water baptism is all that God has for us. But what about the greater works? What about His instruction to *"Heal the sick, raise the dead, cleanse those who have leprosy, drive out demons. Freely you have received; freely give."* (Matt. 10:8).

HE COMMANDED THEM NOT TO GO OUT UNTIL THEY'D RECEIVED THE PROMISE OF THE FATHER. NEITHER CAN WE PRESUME TO SPEAK IN HIS NAME, NOR DO THE WORKS JESUS DID, APART FROM THIS POWER.

Let's look at the day the Spirit of God was poured upon the early Church, giving power to do the signs and miracles we read about. At His departure, Jesus said, *"I am going to send you what my Father has promised; but stay in the city until you have been clothed with power from on high"* (Luke 24:49). He commanded them not to go out until they had received the Promise of the Father. Neither can we presume to speak in His Name, nor do the works Jesus did, apart from this power. It's tragic to ignore or assume you don't need this precious gift of God Himself offered to us!

The Promise of the Father is the Holy Spirit, made available to *all His children* under the New Covenant. Under the Old Covenant, the power of the Spirit came upon only the prophets, priests, and kings who were anointed with oil as a symbol of His outpouring. But God was doing a new thing—under the New Covenant, He shares His Spirit with *all* who believe!

In the last days, God says, I will pour out my Spirit on all people. Your sons and daughters will prophesy, your young men will see visions, your old men will dream dreams. Even on my servants, both men and women, I will pour out my Spirit in those days, and they will prophesy. (Acts 2:17-18; Joel 2:28-29)

How blessed we are that His power can now dwell within and upon every son and daughter! This is the missing element in the lives of many believers today. The Spirit comes to dwell *within us* at salvation, to teach, guide, and enable us for godliness. But the fire is missing—His Spirit *coming upon us* for demonstration of His power, grace, and love. This is the baptism of the Holy Spirit, a second immersion, subsequent to salvation and water baptism. This is why the Apostle Paul spoke of baptisms in plural (Heb. 6:2; 1 Cor. 10:2). See also Acts 8:12-17

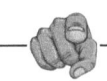

> THE SPIRIT COMES TO DWELL WITHIN US AT SALVATION, TO TEACH, GUIDE, AND ENABLE US FOR GODLINESS. BUT THE FIRE IS MISSING–HIS SPIRIT COMING UPON US FOR DEMONSTRATION OF HIS POWER, GRACE, AND LOVE.

and 10:34-48 for examples of believers who had been water baptized, then baptized in the Holy Spirit at a later time.

Israel as a Prophetic Pattern for Believers

God has painted a beautiful picture of truth to help us see the spiritual progression of believers. It's found in the story of Israel's redemption from slavery into possession of their Promised Land. The Apostle Paul says, *"These things happened to them as examples [types]..."* (1 Cor. 10:11). The Greek word here translated "examples" is *tupos*: a type, pattern, example, model, form *(Strong's Lexicon)*. A "type" is a pattern, or prophetic picture prefiguring a later event. An example is anointing oil as a "type" picturing the outpouring of the Spirit. The following table illustrates some of the types found in the stages of the Israelites' progression from life in Egypt to their Promised Land.

Old Covenant Pattern	New Covenant Experience
Applied the Blood of the Passover Lamb	Jesus, Lamb of God, our Sacrifice slain from the foundation of the world
Exodus from slavery in Egypt	Called out of the "world" & freed from bondage to sin & death
Glory cloud by day & pillar of fire by night	Holy Spirit indwells to lead & protect
1st Baptism: Identified with Moses through waters of Red Sea	Water Baptism: Identify with Christ, dead to old life
Ate manna from Heaven & drank water from the Rock	Jesus, Bread of Life, gives water that never runs dry
Wandered 40 years in Wilderness of Sin	Life of carnal Christian, living for self, never progressing to maturity
Mt. Sinai: Giving of Law written on stone tablets	Mt. Zion: Spirit writes on hearts, Tabernacle of David restored
2nd Baptism: Crossed Jordan River into Promised Land	Baptism of Holy Spirit: Promise of the Father
Circumcision at Gilgal before possession	Circumcision of the heart, cutting off of "flesh", renewal of mind
Consecration to see wonders	Consecrated lives for signs, wonders, miracles
Possession of Promised Land. Victory over enemies.	Walking in the Spirit! Victory! Power for rulership & partnership with God!

The people of Israel wandered around in the Wilderness of Sin for 40 years—uncircumcised of heart, unconsecrated to God, until the last of the unbelieving generation died off. After the issues of circumcision

(Josh. 5:1-9; Deut. 10:12-21) and consecration (Josh. 3:5; 7:1 – 8:1) were addressed, what barrier needed to be overcome to enter into their Promised Land? Crossing the Jordan River! Remember, Jesus, our Pattern, was also baptized at the Jordan and this is when the Dove came to rest upon Him. These events are the prophetic picture of the baptism of the Holy Spirit, the Promise of the Father! A second baptism of living water, when crossed over, gives entrance into a new life—the Promised Land. The same is true today: A river separates the stagnant, old man from the living and flowing spirit of the new man; walking in God's promises or languishing in aimless circles; a dynamic life of power or fear, unbelief, and powerlessness.

A RIVER SEPARATES THE STAGNANT, OLD MAN FROM THE LIVING AND FLOWING SPIRIT IN THE NEW MAN; WALKING IN GOD'S PROMISES OR LANGUISHING IN AIMLESS CIRCLES; A DYNAMIC LIFE OF POWER OR FEAR, UNBELIEF, AND POWERLESSNESS.

Jesus has promised this living water for us!

On the last and greatest day of the festival, Jesus stood and said in a loud voice, "Let anyone who is thirsty come to me and drink. Whoever believes in me, as Scripture has said, rivers of living water will flow from within them." By this he meant the Spirit, whom those who believed in him were later to receive. (John 7:37-39)

The Outpouring of Power

Now we come to the long-awaited day when the Promise of the Father was given! The Passion Translation Bible (TPT) provides a beautiful translation of this event, and the footnotes are very insightful.

EVERY HOLY SPIRIT-BAPTIZED BELIEVER NOW HAS A PILLAR OF FIRE AND GLORY WITHIN AND UPON HIM.

Dr. Brian Simmons, lead translator of the TPT, draws attention to the power found here. He brings to light that every Holy Spirit-baptized believer now has a pillar of fire and glory within and upon him. He also makes clear the difference between being filled inwardly and being equipped for the outflowing of power.

1. *On the day Pentecost was being fulfilled, all the disciples were gathered in one place.*

2. *Suddenly they heard the sound of a violent blast of wind[a] rushing into the house[b] from out of the heavenly realm. The roar of the wind was so overpowering it was all anyone could bear!*

3. *Then all at once a pillar of fire[c] appeared before their eyes. It separated into tongues of fire that engulfed[d] each one of them.*

4. *They were all filled and equipped[e] with the Holy Spirit and were inspired to speak in tongues—empowered by the Spirit to speak in languages they had never learned! (Acts 2:1-4 TPT)*

   a. *2:2 The Aramaic can also be translated "like the roar of a groaning spirit." This mighty wind is for power; the breath of Jesus breathed into His disciples in John 20:22 was for life.*

   b. *2:2 Or "It filled the house." Although most believe this was an upper room, it is possible to conclude from the Aramaic that it was the house of the Lord, (the temple), where they all gathered to celebrate Pentecost. See also Luke 24:53.*

   c. *2:3 This was the pillar of fire that led Israel from bondage into the Promised Land. The same pillar of fire manifested here to initiate a new beginning from dead religious structures into the powerful life of the Spirit. Each believer received an overpowering flame of fire, signified by the shaft of light that engulfed them. It was as though each received his own personal pillar of fire that would empower him and lead him throughout his life. This was the promise Jesus gave to his disciples of "the one like me" (John 14:26), who would be sent by the Father and never leave them. Today every believer is indwelt by the Spirit of Christ (Rom. 8:9). This was the birthday of the church of Jesus Christ.*

d. *2:3 Or "rested" over them.*

e. *2:4 There are two Greek words for "filled..." [One] is pleroo, which means "filled inwardly." In v. 4, it is pletho, which means "filled outwardly" or "furnished and equipped." This was the anointing of the Spirit for ministry. Every believer needs the filling of the Spirit both inwardly for life and outwardly for ministry.*

He wants to "furnish and equip" you, so that you fully possess your Promised Land inheritance in Christ. He wants this power to be activated in your life to validate the message of Christ—this is how we bear witness unto Him, doing His works in His Name. When we do, the Gospel is affirmed and the truth is indisputable.

HE WANTS THIS POWER TO BE ACTIVATED IN YOUR LIFE TO VALIDATE THE MESSAGE OF CHRIST—THIS IS HOW WE BEAR WITNESS UNTO HIM, DOING HIS WORKS IN HIS NAME.

Then the disciples went out and preached everywhere, and the Lord worked with them and confirmed his word by the signs that accompanied it. (Mark 16:20)

The crowds all paid close attention to Philip's message and to the signs they saw him perform. With loud shrieks, unclean spirits came out of many who were possessed, and many of the paralyzed and lame were healed. (Acts 8:6-7)

My message and my preaching were not with persuasive words of wisdom, but with a demonstration of the Spirit's power (1 Cor. 2:4)

WHEN YOU ACCEPT JESUS AS SAVIOR, THAT SAME SPIRIT LIVES WITHIN YOU, FILLING YOU INWARDLY. SEEK YOUR FATHER FOR THE FULLNESS OF HIS PROMISE TO BE "FILLED OUTWARDLY" WITH HIS POWER COMING UPON YOU.

When you accept Jesus as Savior, that same Spirit lives within you, filling you inwardly. Seek your Father for the fullness of His Promise to be "filled outwardly" with His power coming upon you. Jesus assures you that He will do it: *"If you then, though you are evil, know how to give good gifts to your children, how much more will your Father in heaven give the Holy Spirit to those who ask him!"* (Luke 11:13)

Asking and seeking Him for His Promise to be made real in your life—*THAT'S ON YOU!* Pouring His power upon you for signs, wonders, and miracles—*THAT'S ON HIM!*

PART THREE:
PRINCIPLE SCRIPTURES

THAT'S ON
YOU!

PART THREE:
PRINCIPLE SCRIPTURES

The Principles of God

To activate the power of God in your life, you need to live out the principles of God in your life. Sounds simple doesn't it? Not so fast! Remember, life is hard, the devil is real, BUT GOD is good! I recently received a text from a long-time faithful Foundation member that said, "Pastor, what is that thing you say all the time about 'God is good.'" I texted back "LOL Life is hard, the devil is real, BUT GOD is good."

> THE BIBLE CAN BE DESCRIBED AS TWO PARTS: "THE PERSON OF GOD AND THE PRINCIPLES OF GOD." IT'S IMPORTANT NOT TO GLOSS OVER OUR RESPONSIBILITY TO LIVE OUT THE PRINCIPLES OF GOD IN LIFE!

Every time someone is born again at Foundation, I warn them to be ready for the devil to attack. I feel like born-again living should come with warning labels— well, I guess that's the Bible. You know what I mean, warning labels like we see on cigarette packs, alcohol, or prescription medicine. Written (somewhat) in humor, maybe a born-again warning label would read like this: "BEWARE: Born-again living is not for the faint of heart. The enemy has more deceptive ways to attack you than you can imagine. Carry your sword for protection."

God is Faithful and True to His Principles

You learn about both the principles of God and the person of God in the pages of the Bible, which is God's written word. Throughout all the Old and New Testaments, God provides revelation to His people as to how to live out a life that is pleasing to Him. When we live a life that's pleasing to Him, it brings about His blessings and favor. We do our part and He will be sure to do His part—His Name is Faithful and True! (Revelation 3:14; 19:11)

This verse brings back a memory that I think is worth sharing. Back in 1996 when Jennifer and I were first married, I discovered that she was a big fan of Steven Curtis Chapman. She introduced me to the extreme talent and ministry he has. In case you are wondering, yes, I know now, I was late to the party on Steven Curtis Chapman. Better late than never, right?

There is a song about God being Faithful and True that he sings. The lyrics are great! Listen:

"As I look back on the road I've traveled,

I see so many times He carried me through;

and if there is one thing that I've learned in life,

my Redeemer is faithful and true.

And in every situation, He has proved His love to me;

when I lack understanding, He gives more grace to me.

My Redeemer is faithful and true"

(Written by: JAMES ISAAC ELLIOTT, STEVEN CURTIS CHAPMAN

Lyrics © Universal Music Publishing Group)

Go and listen to the whole song, you will be blessed, I am sure. Steven if you're reading this, PLEASE come to Foundation and sing it for us! What the heck, I thought I'd give it a shot and toss an invite out there. LOL!

The reason this song has always blessed me is because no matter how many times I've failed to live out the principles of God in my life, He's always there to provide more grace for me to get back up. Remember, as a follower of Christ, always get back up and try again, because God's grace never runs out. In fact, at Foundation, we expect people to fail, but we are committed to walking with people as they become fully devoted followers of Christ. If you're going to fail at living out the principles of God, then at least fail forward.

Consistently Living His Principles Will Change Your Future

Consistency and persistence can be hard but effective in your pursuit of holy living. Take one of the principles that I will expound on later in the book, "Die to Self." This must happen 365 days a year, 7 days a week, 24 hours a day. I preached a sermon a few years back titled "365/24/7." When you die to self every day, Christ has room to fulfill his plan and purpose in your life. Yes, I said ALL day and EVERY day! The next time someone asked you, "How was your day?" your response should be, "Oh, I died to self probably 25 times today." Well, maybe you shouldn't say that out loud!

I hope you get the point, living out the principles of God is not a some-of-the-time thing; it's an all-the-time-thing. When I think about this, it reminds of what Lamentations 3:22-23 tells us, *"The steadfast love of the Lord never ceases; His mercies never come to an end; they are new every morning; great is thy faithfulness."*

I pray that as we dig into more principles of God throughout this book, that the trajectory of your life will change for the better. Living them out with persistence and consistency in my own life has completely changed the way I think about my future. I no longer think about

GOD IS NO RESPECTER OF PERSONS; HOWEVER, HE IS A RESPECTER OF PRINCIPLES.

- RICHIE MULLIS

my future the way I used to. My dreams have changed. The older I get and the longer I serve the Lord, the more I want to help other people experience that same goodness of God that I have in my life.

In this book, I want to dig deeper into scriptures that give us understanding of the principles of God. We'll call these "principle scriptures". If you've grown up in church or spent any substantial time at a church, these "principle scriptures" will probably be familiar to you. To say the Bible has hundreds would be an understatement. These scriptures provide guidance too, so we can navigate through the ups and downs of life and still experience Christ to the fullest.

Consistently living by God's principles—*THAT'S ON YOU!* Faithfully fulfilling His words of Truth in your life—*THAT'S ON HIM!*

TAKE THE FIRST STEP – THAT'S ON YOU

Thy word is a lamp unto my feet, and a light unto my path. (Psalm 119:105 KJV)

I have heard and read this passage it seems like a thousand times. There is much progress in life to be made through this verse. However, much is required for this kind of progress to come about. The most obvious requirement is that you must take the first step. *THAT'S ON YOU.* The promise is that God's word will provide the lamp and light, but it's on you to take the step.

Why is it that this can be so hard? Well, for starters, the enemy is real, and his desire is for you *not* to take that first step. The devil knows if you take just one step in God's direction, you will experience victory; you will see what is possible when God is in it; you will gain confidence to take a second step, and a third, and a fourth! I call this "spiritual inertia."

Overcome Inertia with the Force of God's Word

Inertia is "a property of matter by which it remains at rest or in uniform motion in the same straight line unless acted upon by some external force…. The inherent property of a body that makes it oppose any force that would cause a change in its motion. A body at rest and a body in motion both oppose forces that might cause acceleration." *(https://www.merriam-webster.com/dictionary/inertia Accessed 24 Dec. 2024)*

Anything spiritual you set in motion in your life tends to stay in motion—by very definition that step will create inertia, which will oppose forces trying to prevent your forward progress. So, go ahead in Jesus' Name and take that first step!

USE THE FORCE OF GOD'S WORD TO OVERCOME THE INERTIA OF A BODY AT REST.

Taking that first step is a move to overcome immobility, stagnation, intimidation, fear, negative thoughts, and more! Use the illumination of God's word to overcome the inertia of a body at rest. It is a lamp and light to guide you in the right direction forward, so you'll be a body in motion.

If you can take just one very small step onto the path God's word illuminates for you, He will do the next thing.

In their hearts humans plan their course, but the LORD establishes their steps. (Proverbs 16:9)

The First Step is the Scariest!

We may believe that God wants what is best for us. We may believe that God has a bright future for us. We may believe that God will empower us. Nevertheless, for some reason taking the first small step can seem like stepping off an extremely high bungee jumping platform. Well, I've actually never bungee jumped before, but it seems kind of scary! I can't stand heights, LOL! It would probably take some encouragement for me to jump.

It can also work like that when taking your first step in the direction that God's word is pointing you in. Fortunately, God specializes in encouragement! Lots of verses come to mind such as, *"He will never leave you nor forsake you"* (Deuteronomy 31:8) or maybe, *"I can do all things through Christ who gives me strength"* (Philippians 4:13).

You don't have to take a giant step. I've learned that God does the big impossible things, if I do the small things. God empowers the small steps that I take in the midst of fear and intimidation, and then He does the divine! He has turned my small steps into bounding leaps! I look back and think to myself, "Only God can do that!"

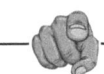

YOU DON'T HAVE TO TAKE A GIANT STEP. I'VE LEARNED THAT GOD DOES THE BIG, IMPOSSIBLE THINGS, IF I DO THE SMALL THINGS.

> *A person's steps are directed by the LORD. How then can anyone understand their own way? (Proverbs 20:24)*

One last thing on this principle verse about God's lamp and light: It's His word that guides you, so *you* must find time to read it or listen to it. A few years ago, my wife and I decided we were going to read the Bible from cover to cover. We committed to one another, along with a few others from our church to do this. WOW! God took us on a journey. His word began to illuminate things to us in a way we hadn't seen before. We ended up reading it two consecutive times over the course of the next year and a half. We continue this practice of reading the Bible together nearly every day. My wife and I were already reading and studying God's word, but something was different about this step we took—and God did the rest! We keep stepping into His word, and He keeps lighting our path for the next step to take. God has blessed us financially, spiritually, and emotionally. We've seen miracles in our lives that only God can perform.

I can't overstate it: Take the first and next step—*THAT'S ON YOU!* If you don't read and meditate on His word, you can't see what God wants to illuminate so you can take the next step.

The LORD makes firm the steps of the one who delights in him; though he may stumble, he will not fall, for the LORD upholds him with his hand. (Psalm 37:23-24)

Making firm your steps and keeping you from falling—*THAT'S ON HIM!*

Applying This Principle–That's on You!

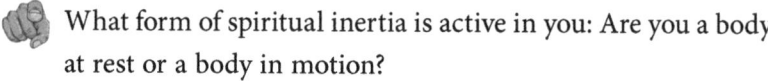 What form of spiritual inertia is active in you: Are you a body at rest or a body in motion?

Can you identify forces at work in your life that would prevent acceleration in your spiritual growth and mobility? What force would set you in motion, and how can you amplify its power in your life?

What did you read that will enable you to overcome immobility? What would slow progression?

What's holding you back from taking the first step?

PRINCIPLE 2
COME TO ME
– THAT'S ON YOU

Come to Me, all you who are weary and heavy burdened, and I will give you rest. Take my yoke upon you and learn from me, for I am gentle and humble in heart, and you will find rest for your souls. (Matthew 11:28-29)

That's on *you*! This is one of the more popular verses of scripture I've heard over the years. As you may have guessed, I want to talk about more in this verse than just receiving "rest" from God. There are actually some things in this verse that we should strive for in order to bring about this "rest" in our lives. Might I dare say, Jesus' words in this verse command you to *learn of Him* and to *obey* in order to experience this kind of rest from God.

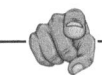

JESUS' WORDS IN THIS VERSE COMMAND YOU TO LEARN OF HIM AND TO OBEY IN ORDER TO EXPERIENCE THE REST OF GOD.

Before diving into what those things are, it's probably a good idea to determine that we all become weary and heavy-burdened at times. Life has a way of bearing down on us. From the unexpected interruptions that we have no way of preparing for, to difficult encounters we have from day-to-day. And that's not all! We have financial burdens, family struggles, issues on our jobs, and more.

This life can be hard to say the least. It's easy to feel weary and burdened. There are seasons in life when we feel more weighed down than anything else. When you experience the weariness and heaviness Jesus described, what should you do?

Only One Can Give True Rest

The very first words of this verse are "Come to me." Have you noticed that at times we tend to run to so many other people or things, before we run to God? We run to addictions, habits, people in power, entertainment, money, jobs and more. You could probably add a few more things to the list. The real point here is that none of these things or people we run to can give us what God can provide. These things are temporary, not eternal. They provide a false sense of rest and satisfaction. They provide small windows of false bravado, distraction, or gratification. They can be based on lies from the enemy that cause you to believe that these temporary things are enough to provide rest.

In reality, there is only ONE person that can give you true rest. I'm talking about the kind of rest that can sustain you, refresh you, and never fail you. You may be thinking, "Yes, that's exactly what I need. Where do I sign up for this kind of rest?"

THE FLESH NEVER FULFILLS THE INNERMOST PARTS OF US. THE FLESH IS ALWAYS IN OPPOSITION TO THE SPIRIT.

Christ makes it easy! No line and no waiting. He simply says, "Come to Me!" Sounds easy, right? Not so fast—remember, we have this thing called "the flesh" to contend with! Our flesh, or the non-spiritual part of us, has a propensity to satisfy *itself.* I can speak from experience when I say that satisfying the flesh never fulfills the innermost parts of us. The flesh is always in opposition to the spirit. So, when you are weary and burdened, you have a choice— *THAT'S ON YOU.* Either run to God or satisfy the flesh. Christ does not make exceptions here! It is for ALL. Your past, your sin, your guilt, your shame. God is saying, "Bring it all with you when you come to Me."

Be Yoked with Jesus

Verse 29 begins with another command: "Take my yoke upon you." I can remember the first time I studied what a "yoke" is. A yoke is a beam or crossbow with reins attached, positioned across the necks of two oxen, so that a farmer can control or guide them. Once the oxen have been trained and are yielded to placement in the yoke, they will respond to the farmer's commands, as a relinquishment of their own will to the farmer's.

According to the experts at Living History Farms, oxen are first trained to listen to the voice of their handlers, or teamsters, and to understand their verbal commands at a young age. They begin to love their handler and will bond with them, looking forward to the petting, grooming, and treats. They learn to wear the yoke and to work as a pair, so that the oxen can work more productively and pull heavier loads. It can take up to four years of training to teach the ox to master the teamster's commands and be most effectual on the farm. (https://www.lhf.org/2015/01/training-new-oxen)

We can easily see the parallels here. Let's put this in a spiritual context: Once we come to Christ, we surrender our wills to His, coming to love and trust Him. He invites us to partner with Him as a team in the yoke. Not only does He give us His added strength to carry our individual burdens in life, He enables us to do His work in greater and greater measure as we grow in maturity.

The Passion Translation provides this footnote for verse 29, "'Bend your neck to my yoke.' The metaphor of a yoke is that it joins two animals to work as one. It is not simply work or toil that is the focus here, but union in Christ." We understand that entering God's "rest" is not the same as

"THE METAPHOR OF A YOKE IS THAT IT JOINS TWO ANIMALS TO WORK AS ONE. IT IS NOT SIMPLY WORK OR TOIL THAT IS THE FOCUS HERE, BUT UNION IN CHRIST."

inactivity; His plan for us is not that we lazily live a life of ease until we go to Heaven and float on a cloud for eternity. He's made us sons and daughters to reign with Him in power and authority, doing His work by the power of His Holy Spirit. We aren't exerting our own strength to work, the energy of the Holy Spirit flows within and from us while we "rest." In this way, we're empowered to do the greater works Jesus told us to do, enabled by His Spirit. (Refer back to Part Two of this book, "Experiencing the Power of God.")

Every step we take, God will be in control. Typically, a yoke is not seen as an instrument of freedom, but this God we serve is not typical. When we take His yoke upon ourselves, He will guide us. God will not lead you to where His providence cannot sustain you.

IT IS MUCH EASIER TO LEARN FROM GOD IF WE ARE ATTACHED TO HIS YOKE AND ARE BEING GUIDED AND DIRECTED BY HIM.

Now let's look at the last thing this verse tells us we must do. It says, "Learn from Me." It is much easier to learn from God if we are attached to His yoke and are being guided and directed by Him. When you attach yourself to things that are not godly, you're running the risk of being led astray from God. There are worldly yokes that lead to bondage and keep you from learning the ways of God. There is the yoke of lust, the yoke of addiction, the yoke of money, the yoke of envy, the yoke of vanity, etc. I could list more but I think you get the point.

We must come to God and choose to take on His yoke, to be able to learn from Him. And, oh yeah, remember, when you do this, He promises that you will find rest for your souls.

Come to God—*THAT'S ON YOU!* Take on His yoke—*THAT'S ON YOU!* Learn from Him—*THAT'S ON YOU!* Providing true freedom and rest—*THAT'S ON HIM!*

Applying This Principle–That's on You!

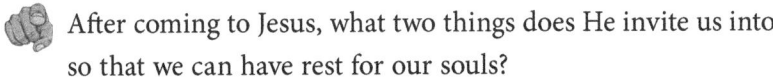 After coming to Jesus, what two things does He invite us into so that we can have rest for our souls?

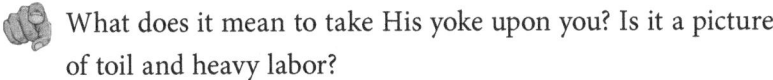 What does it mean to take His yoke upon you? Is it a picture of toil and heavy labor?

As you relinquish your will to His guidance, what will be the outcome? Will it make life and Kingdom service harder or easier?

Read Hebrews 3:7-19 where the writer explains why God angrily swore the people of Israel would never enter His rest. Explain why He was so angry. Verses 14, 15 and 19 of this passage tell us how to avoid this peril so that you can share in Christ by entering His rest:

We have come to share in Christ, if indeed we hold our original conviction firmly to the very end. As has just been said: "Today, if you hear his voice, do not harden your hearts as you did in the rebellion."... So we see that they were not able to enter, because of their unbelief.

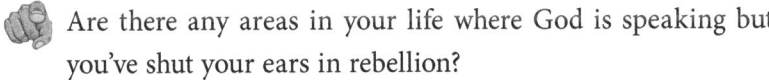 Are there any areas in your life where God is speaking but you've shut your ears in rebellion?

You can make the choice not to harden your heart when you hear His voice, so that you may enter into His rest. You no longer have to walk in weariness and carry heavy burdens! You can walk in freedom and union with Christ as your partner in the yoke!

PRINCIPLE 3
REMAIN IN ME –THAT'S ON YOU

Remain in me, as I also remain in you. No branch can bear fruit by itself; it must remain in the vine. Neither can you bear fruit unless you remain in me. (John15:4)

This verse, in essence, is saying that it is impossible to truly be productive or do good without being connected to God. As Jesus often did, He is trying to teach us this principle by way of a parable. Jesus taught parables to make the principles He was teaching easier to understand. One definition of parable is "a short allegorical story designed to illustrate or teach some truth, or religious principle." In this one, Jesus was teaching the importance of the

"AS YOU LIVE IN UNION WITH ME AS YOUR SOURCE, FRUITFULNESS WILL STREAM FROM WITHIN YOU–BUT WHEN YOU LIVE SEPARATED FROM ME YOU ARE POWERLESS."

- JESUS

union, or covenant attachment, between God and man. The parable He was using illustrates that a branch can only bear fruit when it is attached to a vine. In this instance, Jesus is the Vine, and we are the branches. The branch and the vine must remain attached to each other in order for the branch to bear fruit. He says it this way:

"So you must remain in life-union with me, for I remain in life-union with you. For as a branch severed from the vine will not bear fruit, so your life will be fruitless unless you live your life intimately joined to mine. I am the sprouting vine and you're my branches. As you live in union with me as your source, fruitfulness

will stream from within you—but when you live separated from me you are powerless." (John 15:4-5 TPT)

The Amplified Version renders this passage this way:

"Remain in Me, and I [will remain] in you. Just as no branch can bear fruit by itself without remaining in the vine, neither can you [bear fruit, producing evidence of your faith] unless you remain in Me. I am the Vine; you are the branches. The one who remains in Me and I in him bears much fruit, for [otherwise] apart from Me [that is, cut off from vital union with Me] you can do nothing." (John 15:4-5 AMP)

Nothing is a strong term. Nevertheless, it is what it is—nothing means *nothing*. Let me say it again, apart from God you can do NOTHING.

God's Principles Keep Us in Life-Union with Him

MY UNION WITH CHRIST IS ALWAYS STRONGEST WHEN I AM PUTTING INTO PRACTICE PRINCIPLES THAT I KNOW KEEP ME CONNECTED TO HIM.

As I look back on my own life there is clear evidence of this parable at work. When I stay connected to Jesus, the Vine, I produce fruit. When I disconnect from God, nothing I produce is of any real value. I may be able to produce things of worldly value, but of no eternal value. My union with Christ is always strongest when I am putting into practice principles that I know keep me connected to Him.

For me personally, some of these things include daily Scripture reading, a consistent prayer life, consistent worship habits, reading of devotionals, etc. Without these things in my life, I allow space to come between God and myself. This space that is created allows opportunity for things to fill those empty spaces, causing my union with God to be weakened. The things that create these spaces aren't always bad things. For example, it could be my job, other relationships, hobbies, entertainment, etc. The problem with these things comes when they begin to occupy so much of your time and attention that they cause your relationship with God to suffer. It becomes increasingly difficult to fulfill the principle of "remain in me," or staying attached to the vine. The results or outcomes over time are described in John 15:6: *"If you do not remain in me, you are like a branch that is thrown away and withers; such branches are picked up, thrown into the fire and burned".* Whoa! "Thrown into the fire and burned!" In other words, a life lived that is not attached to the Vine, which is Jesus, has no real value. Some of these things may provide temporary enjoyment or happiness, but eventually, they too will be like a branch that is "thrown into the fire and burned."

To fully live out the principle of "remaining in God" I've had to learn to be more consistent with keeping the main thing, the main thing. I will use the vision statement at Foundation as an example. Our vision is to "Introduce people to Christ and walk with them as they become fully devoted followers." If I'm not careful, I can get more caught up in the "what we are doing" than "why we are doing it," as we fulfil this vision. Let me explain.

There are several ways the people of Foundation make efforts to introduce people to Christ. Examples are passing out invitation cards, sharing social media posts, attending small groups, wearing Foundation church merch, wearing our "Shine Your Light" bracelets, etc. If we're not careful, we can allow *what* we are doing to trump *why* we are doing it. I'm constantly restating our

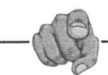

WE'VE REMAINED ATTACHED TO THE VINE, AND HE HAS DECIDED TO REWARD US IN THIS SEASON. HE HAS REWARDED OUR EFFORTS AND STRATEGIES WITH HIS DIVINE SUPERNATURAL POWER, AS WE BEAR MUCH FRUIT.

vision in my sermons, at meetings, and through side conversations, to be sure that the "why" remains rooted in Christ. When we do this, we find that God rewards our faithfulness and maximizes our opportunities to introduce more and more people to Him and fulfill our vision as a church.

As I'm writing this book, our church is experiencing tremendous growth. I'm constantly being asked the question, "What are you doing differently?" My answer is "Really, we aren't doing anything specifically different." We are always trying ways to tell people about Jesus and get them to come to His house. We've remained attached to the Vine, and He has decided to reward us in this season. He has rewarded our efforts and strategies with His divine supernatural power, as we bear much fruit. Not only are we bearing fruit as a church but maybe more importantly, individuals are also bearing fruit. Lives are being changed, families are being changed, marriages are being changed, people are being baptized, and God remains at the center of it all. My prayer is that we never forget to stay attached to the Vine. The Bible clearly tells us that "apart from the Vine we can do nothing."

We Bear Fruit for His Glory

I want to spend a little time looking at the motivating force behind this "remain in me" principle. As we move along in the book of John, we read in verse 8, *"This is to my Father's glory, that you bear much fruit, showing yourselves to be my disciples."* This verse doesn't seem to get the same attention as John 15:4. For all intents and purposes, this verse tells us *why* we should desire to bear fruit. Bearing fruit has more to do with giving God glory than it does anything else.

The evidence of good fruit in our lives is evidence of the goodness of God in our lives. The fruit we produce in our lives is the evidence that we remain attached to the Vine. The evidence of fruit in our lives identifies us as a disciple of Christ. Furthermore, when people partake of the good fruit that we produce through God, they experience God through His Spirit at work in us.

Look at the nine fruits of remaining in union in Jesus that the Apostle Paul mentions in Galatians 5: 22-23: *But the fruit of the Spirit is love, joy, peace, forbearance, kindness, goodness, faithfulness, gentleness and self-control.*

WHEN PEOPLE PARTAKE OF THE GOOD FRUIT THAT WE PRODUCE THROUGH GOD, THEY EXPERIENCE, OR TASTE OF, GOD THROUGH HIS SPIRIT AT WORK IN US.

You can't truly bear this fruit without being attached to the vine. If you're having trouble with forgiveness, remain attached to the vine that will produce it for you. The same goes for any of these. Attach to the vine and the vine will produce what you are incapable of producing on your own. The fruit of the Spirit are beneficial for you and the people who partake of it, because it is working through you. And in the end, it all glorifies God.

Whatever good fruit you are trying to produce the Lord can provide; He will produce it within you—*THAT'S ON HIM.* His name is Jehovah Jireh, The Lord Our Provider. Remaining in vital life-union with Him—*THAT'S ON YOU!*

Applying This Principle—That's on You!

 What is Jesus revealing to us in the parable of the Vine?

 What is the outcome for a branch detached from the Vine?

 Are you living in life-union with Him? What things can you do to live more fully aware of your covenant attachment to the Vine?

What is the purpose of bearing fruit? Are you fruitful?

Read Psalm 15 and understand the etiquette for those who would dwell in the shining place of God's glory. Encourage yourself to live in this way so you will remain in Him. What could be better?!

PRINCIPLE 4

DEVELOP YOUR FRIENDSHIP WITH GOD – THAT'S ON YOU

"You are my friends if you do whatever I command you" (John 15:14)—*THATS ON YOU!* It's up to you to choose what level of relationship you want to have with God. An old-time preacher named R.W. Schambach used to sing a song with the chorus that said, "I know God is God, and God don't ever change." I know the lyrics aren't grammatically correct, but they hit different when said that way. As I look back through the years and reflect on my friendship with God, it can truly be said that "God don't ever change."

Hebrews 13:8 tells us, *"Jesus Christ the same yesterday, and today, and forever."* I'm so thankful for this verse. This tells me that I can depend on God in my friendship with Him. Life may change, careers may change, the world may change, but God *NEVER* changes. With as much uncertainty that life

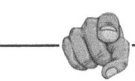

THE LEVEL OF RELATIONSHIP YOU WANT TO HAVE WITH GOD IS UP TO YOU.

can bring, especially in our relationships, it's good to know that God is not the author of uncertainty.

Who Are We that He Should Call Us Friends?

There is an interesting shift that takes place after John 15:14, as in verse 15 Jesus says, *"I no longer call you slaves, because a master doesn't confide in his slaves. Now you are my friends, since I have told you everything the Father told me."* What a joy it is to know that God considers us His friends. There are scriptures scattered throughout the Bible that describe God as being a friend:

Inside the Tent of Meeting, the LORD would speak to Moses face to face, as one speaks to a friend. (Exodus 33:11a NLT)

Abraham believed God, and God counted him as righteous because of his faith, He was even called the friend of God. (James 2:23 NLT)

Can you believe that the Creator of man, the Creator of Heaven and Earth, the Giver of salvation, allows us to be His friends? This is a big deal! So how do we become a friend of God? Are we friends right away, when we give our hearts to him? My answer to this is that we are inherently His children first and then we develop a friendship with God in time. It's like this in some of our families too: Some children are on very familiar terms with their father, while others rarely spend close time with them and don't know their hearts or activities.

THERE ARE MANY LIKE US, BUT ONLY ONE GOD SO KIND AND WILLING TO SUSTAIN DIFFICULT FRIENDSHIPS.

I've found my relationship with God has developed by spending intimate time with Him in prayer. I've come to know God in a deeper, more personal way by talking to Him and listening to His voice speak to me. The word intimate means a "very close friend or a constant companion." This constant companionship I have with God has caused my friendship to grow more and more over the years.

I've thought about the personal friendship I have with God, and about how imbalanced it is from a give and take standpoint. God has always been good to me, but I have not always obeyed. God has always loved me, even when I was not very lovable. God has always picked me up when I was down. Trust me when I say, there have been many times when I was down, and God did a lot of "picking up." Outside of God, a relationship so imbalanced would not be able to withstand the test of time. But God is different! There are a lot like us, but only one God so kind and willing to sustain difficult friendships. When my relationship with God has suffered, it was because I didn't live up to my side of the relationship and had difficulty keeping His commands.

Make Spending Time with Him Intentional

Like any other friendship, you need to make time for your relationship with God. There are several ways I spend time with God.

1. I spend daily time in prayer. This is time for just God and me, our intimate time together. I carve time out in my day to make this happen. I do this 365 days a year, multiple times a day.

2. I spend time in praise and worship. This could be just God and me or in a group setting. I do this a lot in my office; I do this at Church; I do this in my car.

3. I spend time in Scripture. This time could be me alone or maybe with my wife Jennifer. My wife and I have made it a daily practice to do this together. It has been life-changing. I highly recommend reading your Bible together with your spouse.

4. I spend time in a small group. This is typically with a group of church folks. For many years, I undervalued small groups.

5. I spend time preparing sermons. This is kind of a 24/7 thing for a pastor. I love writing sermons and preaching. It is probably the most enjoyable thing I do in ministry. I tell people who are around me, "You are always subject to be an example in my next sermon." My family knows this all too well!

6. I spend time on the treadmill—I meditate and put on some of my go-to worship songs. This is my decompression time. I usually walk for one hour; no TV and no talking to others. Just me and my Jesus music. In case you are wondering who is on my playlist when it comes to worship, my list includes: Kim Walker-Smith, NEEDTOBREATHE, Maverick City, Forrest Frank, Elevation, and We The Kingdom, to name a few.

My list of ways to spend time with God, may look different than yours. Maybe you don't have a list at all. If that is you, there is no better time than today to carve out intentional time to spend with God.

Conviction's Role in Friendship with God

KEEP IN MIND, FRIENDSHIP IS TWO-WAY, NOT ONE-WAY. IN A RELATIONSHIP, ONE PERSON CAN'T DO ALL THE TALKING.

Conviction is not typically the first thing you think of regarding friendship with God. Keep in mind, friendship is two-way, not one-way. In a relationship, one person can't do all the talking. That really isn't much of a relationship; it's an unhealthy one at best. As your relationship with God grows, you'll learn to recognize God's voice and the many ways He speaks to you. This takes time, because the voice of God is generally not audible or out loud.

After years of serving God, I can say that He initiates a lot of the conversations I have with Him. Jesus said, *"My sheep hear my voice, and I know them, and they follow me..."* (John 10:27 NKJV). He guides me, leads me, and shows me the way.

I can remember when I learned that one of the ways He speaks is with the voice of conviction. The Bible says in Romans 8:1, *Therefore, there is now no condemnation for those who are in Christ Jesus.* It does *not* say that there is now no *conviction.* I've learned through the spiritual maturation process that conviction is a good thing. I've become more and more aware of the goodness of God and of just how sinful my human nature is. Speaking of the Holy Spirit, Jesus said, *"And when He comes, He will convict the world of its sin..."* (John 16:8a NLT). It is conviction that makes us aware of our sin by showing us what it is, and how it grieves and quenches His Spirit, leading us to repent of that sin. Conviction causes you to change the way you talk, the

CONVICTION CAUSES YOU TO CHANGE THE WAY YOU TALK, THE WAY YOU THINK, THE WAY YOU TREAT OTHERS, AND EVEN THE WAY YOU THINK ABOUT YOURSELF.

way you think, the way you treat others, and even the way you think about yourself. When you first come to Jesus, it's by way of conviction. God's voice causes you realize the depths of your depravity and sin. You realize that the blood of His substitutionary sacrifice and salvation in Jesus Christ is the only thing that can make you pure and holy.

Friendship with God through His Written Word

There are many times people tell me, "Pastor, I just haven't been hearing from God." My typical answer to them is with a question. I ask, "Are you reading you Bible?" This happens a lot with new believers. I always tell new believers to find an easy-to-understand version of the Bible and start reading it. My most preferred versions of the Bible are NIV, NLT, and sometimes only the good ole KJV will do. I suggest new believers start with the simpler books, maybe the Gospels, Psalms, and Proverbs. In my years of ministry, there have been so many people who try to start in Genesis and read forward from there. There is nothing wrong with this, but if you think a new believer can make their way through Leviticus, Numbers and Deuteronomy, with the same ease as Matthew, Mark, Luke, and John, you're sadly mistaken. If I'm going to try to help them develop their relationship with God, I want them to be successful.

Recognizing the Voice of Your Friend

Back in the fall of 2010 when God was speaking to Jennifer and me about planting a church, there were several challenges. One of the challenges we would often talk about is where the new church would be located. I remember calling my friend Tony Byrd in Tampa Bay, Florida, who had just planted MorningStar Church. Among my list of questions for Tony was, "How did you know that Tampa was where God wanted you to plant?" Tony responded by saying, "Scott, I know you may think this is just cliché, but you have to pray about it".

At the time, I was like "LOL Tony, I appreciate that." Looking back, what did I think Tony was going to say? Did I really think he was going to say, "That's easy Scott, God told me in me in a loud booming voice to plant the church in Tampa."

In the coming months, Foundation started hosting what we called preview services. We hosted three of these preview services every other month over a six-month period. These services were hosted at the local school district where our current facility is located in Trenton, Ohio. The space was available at a reasonable price, and it made sense at the time. However, I was a bit unfamiliar with the area, feeling it was lower in population and wouldn't give us the traffic we needed to grow. I know what you must be thinking, if God is in it, He will send the people. Yes! That is true, but my "business" thinking was trumping my spiritual thinking at the time.

It finally came time for us to host weekly services in the fall of 2011. Our preview services were averaging 20-40 people at the time. Jennifer and I were still asking, "Where are we going to host our weekly services?" That is when it hit us! FOUNDATION MUST STAY

IN TRENTON. We clearly recognized God's voice and the answer to our prayers that my friend Tony had spoken to me about. We now understood that the 20-40 people God had sent us during those preview services were our congregation, and they considered us to be their pastors. The reality is, all along God was trying to speak to me, but I wasn't hearing Him clearly. My ability to hear God's voice was being clouded by my own ideas of where I thought Foundation would be located. The part that I was hearing correctly was that God was calling me to

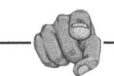

HAD I NOT RECOGNIZED HIS VOICE BECAUSE OF MY FRIENDSHIP WITH HIM, WHO KNOWS WHAT THE FUTURE OF THE CHURCH WOULD HAVE LOOKED LIKE? OR IF THERE WOULD HAVE BEEN ANY FUTURE FOR THE CHURCH AT ALL!

plant a church, and by His grace I responded in faith. That was on me! However, I was missing the mark on where I was supposed to plant the church. Had I not recognized His voice because of my friendship with Him, who knows what the future of the church would have looked like? Or if there would have been any future for the church at all!

One who has unreliable friends soon comes to ruin, but there is a friend who sticks closer than a brother. (Proverbs 18:24)

God being a reliable friend that sticks closer than a brother—*THAT'S ON HIM!* Developing intimate friendship with God and learning to know His voice—*THAT'S ON YOU!*

Applying This Principle–That's on You!

 Read John 15:14 at the beginning of this chapter. Do you see yourself in the role of a slave or servant, or as a friend of God?

 Do you have a close and personal relationship with your Father in Heaven? What things can you apply to deepen it, regardless of your current level of intimacy with Him?

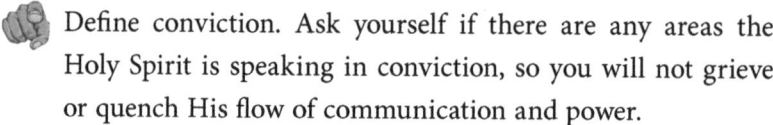 Define conviction. Ask yourself if there are any areas the Holy Spirit is speaking in conviction, so you will not grieve or quench His flow of communication and power.

Reread John 10:27: *"My sheep hear my voice, and I know them, and they follow me..."* Do you recognize the voice of your Friend? How might you hear Him more clearly, so that you can follow more closely? He wants to lead you into green pastures where you'll find refreshing rest for your soul!

There's a private place reserved for the lovers of God, where they sit near Him and receive the revelation-secrets of His promises. (Psalm 25:14 TPT)

Do you make time to sit with Him and hear His secrets? He will reveal them to you!

PRINCIPLE 5
KEEP MY COMMANDS – THAT'S ON YOU

If you love me, keep my commands. (John 14:15)

Wow, that's tough! In order to show my love for God, I must keep His commands. Maybe you are thinking, I indeed love God and I want to get started on this right away, so where do I find this list of commands? Do we still have a fresh tablet of the commands that God gave to Moses for us to keep? Maybe I'll start with those. Or, can I do a quick Google search without even getting off the couch — that would make it easy. Ok, ok, surely, they will have a huge stack of these commands at the church, in a back room somewhere.

He Writes on the Tablets of Hearts

Let me help you, you'll be looking a long time for a specific list. Newsflash: you won't find a list! Yes, I know the ten commandments are in the Bible, but there are many more than those given to us from Moses. In fact, some commands haven't even been given to you yet! Think about that, commands that haven't even been spoken into existence yet! How can that be? First, you must understand how

SOME COMMANDS HAVEN'T EVEN BEEN GIVEN TO YOU YET! THINK ABOUT THAT, COMMANDS THAT HAVEN'T EVEN BEEN SPOKEN INTO EXISTENCE YET, THAT GOD WILL SPEAK TO YOU!

God speaks His commands into existence every day. The Bible tells us exactly where these commands can be found. Let me give you two scriptures:

You yourselves are our letter, written on our hearts, known and read by everyone. You show that you are a letter from Christ, the result of our ministry, written not with ink but with the Spirit of the living God, not on tablets of stone but on tablets of human hearts. (2 Corinthians 3:2-3)

I will put new laws into their minds and write them on their hearts... (Hebrews 8:10b)

HIS COMMANDS ARE WRITTEN ON OUR HEARTS. AS WE WALK DAILY WITH GOD, HE INFORMS US OF WHAT IS THE RIGHT THING TO DO BY WAY OF THE HEART.

So, there is the answer, that's where you find the commands of God. His commands are written on our hearts. As we walk daily with God, He informs us of what is the right thing to do by way of the heart. This is why it's paramount that you give your heart to God. When you give your heart to God, it softens your heart, and you become sensitive to God, with the ability to hear His voice as He speaks to you. Jesus said, *"My sheep listen to my voice; I know them, and they follow me"* (John 10:27).

Sometimes when God speaks to you, it is with a command, by way of the Spirit living within you. Obeying the Sprit when He speaks is always the right thing to do. You must get your heart aligned with God. I often hear people quote Psalm 37:3, *"God will give you the desires of your heart."* I always follow that up with, "Well then, you better make sure your heart is lined up with the things of God."

God's Commands Specific to *You*

As a pastor, I get many questions about what a sin is, or what is not a sin, as if I am the keeper of "the list" of sins. I know why folks ask me this—it's because they're grappling with a command that God is trying to write on their heart. I am not God and can't write anything on someone's heart. So, I usually respond in a couple of different ways. One way I respond is to ask the person, "What is the Spirit of God telling you about it?" A second way I could respond may be, "Why are you asking?"

My goal when people ask me questions about sin is to get them to engage with God about the matter through prayer. I tell them, God will never lead you in the wrong direction about sin.

In all your ways acknowledge Him and He shall direct your path. (Proverbs 3:6)

And whether you turn to the right or to the left, your ears will hear this command behind you: "This is the way. Walk in it." (Isaiah 30:21)

Keeping Gods commands is not a behavior modification program. In many ways, keeping God's commands is about the journey of life with God as He allows you to perfect your faith over time and to live a life fully devoted to Him. This way of living is very individualized and specific to you. On this journey, you will have failures, as well as successes. Why does God allow you to fail? Because on this journey, sometimes we learn best through failure. Failure has a unique way of bringing us to our knees and causing us to fully

KEEPING GOD'S COMMANDS IS ABOUT THE JOURNEY OF LIFE WITH GOD AS HE ALLOWS YOU TO PERFECT YOUR FAITH OVER TIME.

surrender ourselves to God. In these moments of surrender, our hearts become softened, and God can write His commands on our hearts.

Always remember, failure is not final. Failure does not define you. Allow God to work through your failures to make you more like him. Following His commands and becoming more like Him keeps us on the narrow path to our destiny. The path is narrow because God does not allow for compromise. His commands are His *commands*. Holy living is *living holy*. Line your life up with what the Word of God says and with God's commands for *you*.

God will always speak to you and write His will on your heart, giving you commands and direction to fulfill His perfect plan for you— *THAT'S ON HIM!* Keeping His commands—*THAT'S ON YOU!*

Applying This Principle–That's on You!

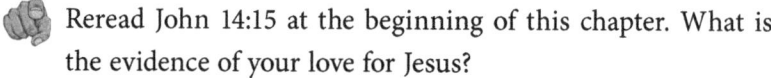 Reread John 14:15 at the beginning of this chapter. What is the evidence of your love for Jesus?

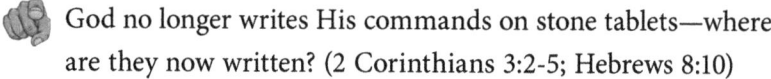 God no longer writes His commands on stone tablets—where are they now written? (2 Corinthians 3:2-5; Hebrews 8:10)

Apart from the unchangeable principles found in His Word, God's New Covenant commands are specific to you. What's OK for someone else may not be OK for you. Read the following passage.

One person's faith allows them to eat anything, but another, whose faith is weak, eats only vegetables. The one who eats everything must not treat with contempt the one who does not, and the one who does not eat everything must not judge the one who does, for God has accepted them. Who are you to judge someone else's servant? To their own master, servants stand or fall.... I am convinced, being fully persuaded in the Lord Jesus, that nothing is unclean in itself. But if anyone regards something as unclean, then for that person it is unclean. So whatever you believe about these things keep between yourself and God. Blessed is the one who does not condemn himself by what he approves. But whoever has doubts is condemned if they eat, because their eating is not from faith; and everything that does not come from faith is sin. (Romans 14:2-4; 14; 22-23)

Ask yourself: Are there any areas the Holy Spirit is speaking specifically to me which I'm resisting? Am I comparing myself to someone else to whom God is not speaking about this?

Am I judging someone else who may not have the same conviction, or command from God?

PRINCIPLE 6
SOWING SEED – THAT'S ON YOU

Providing the harvest is on God. This sounds so simple, but sowing seed can be very difficult to grapple with in our natural minds. Sowing seed is a spiritual decision that requires a great deal of faith. Any seed that is planted has to be released from our hand. As you may know, there are some things in our lives that we don't want to let go of. Whatever that thing is in your life, it eventually has to go from your hand into fertile ground. You eventually have to depend on God to provide. You eventually have to walk away and believe that God will cause the seed to return a harvest.

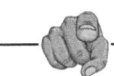

I'VE FOUND THAT PEOPLE HAVE MORE FAITH THAT GRASS WILL SPROUT FROM GRASS SEED THAN TO BELIEVE THAT SPIRITUAL SEEDS PLANTED WILL GROW AND RETURN A HARVEST.

I've found that people have more faith that grass will sprout from grass seed than to believe the spiritual seeds planted will grow and return a harvest. One of God's spiritual laws is that you will reap what you sow. You can't change this! If the Bible says it, then it's a fact. This is one of God's first principles, as seen in the first chapter of the Bible.

Then God said, "Let the land produce vegetation: seed-bearing plants and trees on the land that bear fruit with seed in it, according to their various kinds." And it was so. The land produced vegetation: plants bearing seed according to their kinds and trees bearing fruit with seed in it according to their kinds. And God saw that it was good. (Genesis 1:11-12)

> YOU DON'T HAVE THE ATTRIBUTES OF GOD TO PRODUCE THE HARVEST, BUT I BELIEVE HE HAS GIVEN YOU THE ABILITY TO INFLUENCE THE HARVEST.

Although you don't have the attributes of God to *produce* the harvest, I believe He has given you the ability to *influence* the harvest. I believe you can influence what you harvest and how much you will harvest. For example, if you continually sow many seeds of goodness into other people's lives, you will reap lots of goodness in your own life at just the right time.

Here's another example: If you sow financial seed into the Kingdom of God, you will receive a financial harvest at just the right time.

Patience is Needed after Sowing Seed

Let me explain to help you understand what I am saying a little better. If you sow lots of grass seed, you will reap lots of grass at just the right time. You don't wake up the next morning with a yard full of grass. Notice I am using the phrase "at just the right time."

When I was a boy growing up in church, there was a song we used to sing with the chorus,

He's an on-time God— yes, He is!
He may not come when you want,
but He will always come on time.
He's an on-time God— yes, He is!

This is true with sowing and reaping. You may have been waiting a long time to reap a harvest from the seeds that you have been planting. You must remember that God knows what you don't know and can see what you cannot see. By faith, you must believe that He will provide the harvest at just the right time. Waiting on the harvest is always filled with great anticipation.

Reaping the harvest is also highly connected to God's timing. I once heard it said, "The harvest is the hardest part." Let me explain— I would love to see my congregation at Foundation triple in size this coming Sunday. What a great harvest, manifested from the seeds of faith that have been planted! Unfortunately, if that happened this week, I am not sure our church has the infrastructure or physical capacity to serve that many people right now.

God Knows our Time for Reaping

Perhaps God is still preparing you to receive what it is that He wants to provide, but you aren't prepared to receive it all without squandering it. You must keep the same faith while you are waiting on the harvest that you had when you planted the seed.

Jesus also said, "The Kingdom of God is like a farmer who scatters seed on the ground. Night and day, while he's asleep or awake, the seed sprouts and grows, but he does not understand how it happens. The earth produces the crops on its own. First a leaf blade pushes through, then the heads of wheat are formed, and finally the grain ripens. And as soon as the grain is ready, the farmer comes and harvests it with a sickle, for the harvest time has come." (Mark 4:26-28 NLT)

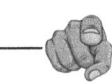

YOU MUST KEEP THE SAME FAITH WHILE YOU ARE WAITING ON THE HARVEST THAT YOU HAD WHEN YOU PLANTED THE SEED.

Causing the seed to grow and bear fruit—*THAT'S ON GOD!* Releasing it from your hand and waiting in faith to reap the harvest— *THAT'S ON YOU!*

Applying This Principle—That's on You!

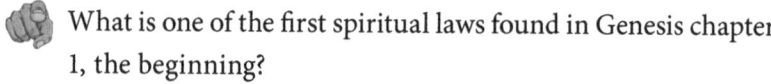 What is one of the first spiritual laws found in Genesis chapter 1, the beginning?

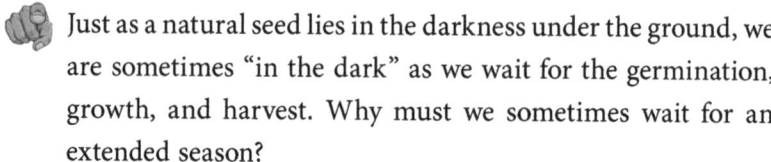 Just as a natural seed lies in the darkness under the ground, we are sometimes "in the dark" as we wait for the germination, growth, and harvest. Why must we sometimes wait for an extended season?

Read the passage near the end of the chapter (Mark 4:26-28). Note that while the farmer goes about his business and sleeps, the seed sprouts and grows, though he doesn't know how. The earth, or the God-provided environment of cultivation, does it on its own. How can this understanding be applied to Kingdom sowing and reaping?

PRINCIPLE 7
GROW
– THAT'S ON YOU

The concept of growing in God is one that speaks to where someone may be on their "Christian continuum." I've referenced this term many times over the years! I feel like God put it into my spirit probably twenty years ago. The word "continuum" is defined as "a coherent whole characterized by the progression of values." When you attach the word "Christian" to the word continuum, you get a picture of what a typical Christ-follower's life looks like over time.

God's Grace Promotes Growth

Let me explain. On some days you feel like you've made a great deal of progress in your walk with God, while on other days you may feel like you've regressed in your walk with Him. Christian progress over the course of time is easier to see, rather than trying to gauge your progress on the outcomes of a single day. I always describe one's Christian continuum as a sliding scale, meaning you may not feel like much growth is taking place in your relationship with God, but when you look back over time, you can clearly see that you've grown. How does this happen? To put it as simply as I can, it's because of the grace of God in your life. God's grace promotes continual growth over time.

But grow in the grace and knowledge of our Lord and Savior Jesus Christ. (2 Peter 3:18a)

ONE OF THE UNDERESTIMATED FACTORS IN BEING ABLE GROW IN GOD'S GRACE IS TIME.

You can look back and say, "I'm not the same person I used to be." One of the underestimated factors in being able grow in God's grace is time. Sometimes we forget to tell new believers that they are babies in Christ. We must remember to emphasize to new believers that they've been born again. Being born again means you must learn how to walk and live this new life you've been given. This means many of the things that worked for you in your old life may not work in your new life.

Therefore, if anyone is in Christ, the new creation has come: The old has gone, the new is here! (2 Corinthians 5:17)

Like newborn babies, crave pure spiritual milk, so that by it you may grow up in your salvation, now that you have tasted that the Lord is good. (1 Peter 2:2-3)

Many people give their hearts to God, pull up to His table, and order steak and potatoes. For these folks maybe there is a spiritual Heimlich maneuver. Peter tells us, as babies in Christ, to "crave spiritual milk." As you grow older, maybe then you will be ready for the steak and potatoes.

These are some questions to ask yourself if you are a brand-new believer that will help you progress on your Spiritual Continuum:

1. Do I have an easy-to-understand Bible that I can read?

2. Do I have a routine that will allow me to devote time to pray to God?

3. Have I found a good Bible-based church to attend, where I can grow and learn?

These questions to help you progress on your Spiritual Continuum will be slightly different if you're a more mature believer:

4. Is my Bible knowledge continuing to deepen as I spend daily time in God's word?

5. Is my prayer life and intimacy with God continuing to deepen over time?

6. Am I devoting my time, talent, and treasure in a good Bible-based church?

Learn how to take baby steps and drink all the "spiritual milk" you can get. Eventually you will graduate to "spiritual baby food" and then "spiritual whole foods." Are you noticing a progression here? You can't skip any steps, to grow, you must learn.

Go back to the scripture I referenced from 2 Peter 3:18: "But grow in the grace..." The grace of God is what allows you to grow in the knowledge of God. Let's take this a step further and include the mercy of God. Maybe you've heard it said before that "the grace of God gives you what you don't deserve, and the mercy of God keeps you from what you do deserve." When you put the mercy of God with the grace of God together, growing in God is inevitable. The prophet Jeremiah said that God's mercies are new every morning. Wow! That means that by His grace, when the morning comes, nothing you did yesterday can keep you from spiritual growth because of God's mercy.

The faithful love of the LORD NEVER ENDS! HIS MERCIES NEVER CEASE. Great is his faithfulness; his mercies begin afresh each morning. (Lamentations 3:22-23 NLT)

If this were a math equation, maybe it would read like this:

GRACE + MERCY + KNOWLEDGE = SPIRITUAL GROWTH

Keep in mind, it's on you to live this way. You don't have to accept the grace of God. You don't have to take advantage God's mercy. You don't have to pursue more knowledge about who God is and what He has done for you!

I was once told that "healthy things grow." When I first heard it, I jotted it down in the Note's app on my phone. (That's where I put things that I don't want to forget.) At some point in time, I went back to that note and began to give it spiritual context. Then as you may have guessed, I developed a sermon series entitled "Healthy Things Grow." I want to share a few of my main points from that series, in hopes it will give you some real-world application.

1. Environment Influences Growth

FOR A CHRIST-FOLLOWER TO GROW, WE MUST CREATE AN ENVIRONMENT IN OUR LIVES THAT ALLOWS FOR SPIRITUAL GROWTH.

Any living thing has a preferred environment that is most suitable for optimal growth. An example of an environment that influences growth would be how a cactus grows best in the desert. A cactus grows best in light, heat, and with the proper rate of drainage. To avoid boring you with how to best create an environment to grow cacti, I will just say that they are unique plants that require a different kind of care than many other plants. The same goes with followers of Christ. For a Christ-follower to grow, we must create an environment in our lives that allows for spiritual growth. This may mean changing friends, changing where you hang out, changing what you listen to, changing what you watch, or changing your routines.

2. Growing Things Change

If we believe that healthy things grow, we must acknowledge that growing things change. God's Word correlates this kind of change with being dead to sin, then being made alive in Christ! You are no longer who you used to be. Just like a seed that is planted will eventually no longer be a seed, but will become whatever it was created to become, grass seed becomes grass when planted in the right environment. You should always be striving to become who you are created to be in Christ. You must expect change to happen in your life if you want to grow spiritually. You may even change the way you think about your future. Simply put, growing means you will constantly be in a process of change.

3. Growing Things Require Nourishment

We make great progress on the Christian continuum when we realize that we become alive in Christ when we are born again. We begin to nourish the new creation. One way to nourish the new creation is through the reading of God's Word. This is just one of many ways to nourish ourselves spiritually. When you nourish the spirit, the spirit will grow. When you do this daily, you can experience rapid spiritual growth.

Man shall not live by bread alone, but by every word that proceeds from the mouth of God. (Matthew 4:4b NKJV)

4. Seasons Influence Growth

If you neglect the necessary approach that each season of life requires, you will cheat the potential that exists in the next season.

Obedience as a pathway to spiritual and personal growth is a recurring theme throughout the Bible, and as the truism says, we grow at the speed of our obedience.

> *Let us not grow weary or become discouraged in doing good, for at the proper time we will reap, if we do not give in. (Galatians 6:9 AMP)*

There are tons of scripture in the Bible about the seasons of life. I've struggled in certain seasons of life, while being able to celebrate in other seasons. I've learned over time to be patient and trust that there will be greater days ahead in the next season. When I trust that God's timing is better than mine, I grow. When I trust that God can see what I cannot see, I grow. Listen up! If you could see what God sees, you would wait differently! Don't grow weary—in the proper time, or "due season", you will reap! You can only reap a harvest in one season because you were able to grow in the previous season.

Setting yourself up for spiritual growth—*THAT'S ON YOU!* Providing the spiritual harvest for you to reap—*THAT'S ON GOD!*

Applying This Principle—That's on You!

 What two things does the Apostle Peter encourage us to grow in? (2 Peter 3:18)

 Where are you on your Spiritual Continuum? Look back at the corresponding questions and determine if you're setting yourself up for progress.

 Are you living in the right environment to promote spiritual growth? Are you in the place God has determined you be planted?

Are you providing yourself with rich spiritual nourishment?

Taste and see that the LORD is good; blessed is the one who takes refuge in him. (Psalm 34:8)

PRINCIPLE 8
DO NOT FEAR
– THAT'S ON YOU

God did not give you a Spirit of fear. Along with experiencing the power of God in your life, overcoming fear is on you! *God has given you a spirit of power, and of love, and of a sound mind.* (2 Timothy 1:7) Sounds so simple, doesn't it? Well, living this verse out in your day-to-day life can be difficult to say the least.

I've known people who walk in fear every day, sometimes all day, every day. The enemy has been able to sneak into the corners of their mind and plant seeds of fear. Keep in mind that seeds grow if you water them. We must learn to do what the Bible says in 2 Corinthians 10:4: *We take every thought captive and make it obedient to Christ.* When we do this, we can exhibit divine power to destroy strongholds such as fear in our lives.

In my own life, I've learned to be on the lookout for divine revelation from God as a means of overcoming fear. For me, divine revelation often comes by way of the voice of God speaking to me. Over time, I've come to know His voice and how He speaks. He may speak through an open door, a closed door, or possibly through an opportunity that requires faith on my side of the covenant that I have with Him.

BE ON THE LOOKOUT FOR DIVINE REVELATION FROM GOD AS A MEANS OF OVERCOMING FEAR.

Seeds of Fear Grow When Watered

What happens when we do not take every thought captive and make it obedient to Christ? One outcome could be that we give those thoughts of fear space to grow in our minds. It's your mind that the enemy is really after. If He can get you to believe or fear something, he can influence your decisions and behaviors. This is what the enemy did in the Garden when he asked Eve, "Did God really say what you think He said...surely you won't die," (See Genesis 3:3-4.) That was enough! The seed was planted in Eve's mind and she watered it!

When you think deeply about fear, you realize that fear is not a tangible thing. Fear is simply a thought about something that we believe may happen. Think for a second about how you would describe fear to someone. The existence of fear is a hard thing to describe, because it's not tangible. However, it is real enough to paralyze parts of our lives, and the thing we fear hasn't even materialized.

Fear is in our present mind but the thing we fear is in the future. It could be in the very near future, or in the very distant future. Often, what we fear never comes to be. Jesus said in Matthew 6:34, *"Therefore do not worry about tomorrow, for tomorrow will worry about itself. Each day has enough trouble of its own."* This doesn't mean that we neglect proactive planning and being good stewards of the things God has provided in our lives. But it could indicate that we need to exercise a greater level of faith and stewardship of the blessings that God has placed in our lives.

LIVE IN A WAY THAT SHOWS YOU BELIEVE THAT GOD IS GOING TO PROTECT AND SUSTAIN YOU NO MATTER WHAT YOU FEAR.

Live in a way that shows you believe that God is going to protect and sustain you no matter what you fear. The Bible says in Hebrews 13:5 that *God will never leave you or forsake you.* You must learn to meditate much on scriptures like these and even commit them to memory, so that they become hidden in your heart. This is a great spiritual tool for you to use.

God's Truth Defeats Fear

The Apostle Paul describes this spiritual weapon as the Truth of God's Word, "the sword of the Spirit" (Ephesians 6:17). The Holy Spirit will bring His living Word to your mind so that you can stand firm and cut down every thought of fear that opposes it. Scripture has more to say about this weapon:

> For though we live in the world, we do not wage war as the world does. The weapons we fight with are not the weapons of the world. On the contrary, they have divine power to demolish strongholds. We demolish arguments and every pretension that sets itself up against the knowledge of God, and we take captive every thought to make it obedient to Christ. (2 Corinthians 10:3-5)

> For the word of God is alive and active. Sharper than any **double-edged sword** [emphasis added], it penetrates even to dividing soul and spirit, joints and marrow; it judges the thoughts and attitudes of the heart. (Hebrews 4:12)

Note that Scripture refers to it as a **two-edged sword** (Hebrews 4:12; Psalm 149:6-9; Isaiah 41:15). The sword of the Spirit must come from our mouths; this is the way its power is released. *Jesus speaks*, then *we speak* what He says–that is "two-mouthed," or double-edged. A sword is useless unless it is taken up and used against your enemy. When we're faced with fear (or any enemy of our souls), we must take up the two-mouthed sword of the Spirit and speak His Word over our thoughts, minds, situations, etc. That is both your defensive and offensive weapon—take it out of its sheath and speak God's powerful, living truth!

The next time the enemy tries to build a stronghold of fear in your mind, demolish it with "the sword of truth." Saying what the Spirit says—*THAT'S ON YOU!* Making it powerful over every enemy that comes against you—*THAT'S ON GOD!*

Applying This Principle–That's on You!

In opposition to fear, what kind of spirit has God given you? (See 2 Timothy 1:7)

What are some outcomes of allowing fear to build a stronghold in your mind? How do you demolish it?

Read Luke 12:22-31 where Jesus teaches on fear and worry. What is the people-group who give themselves to worry? How does He describe their faith level? How can you build your faith? (Romans 10:17)

What spiritual weapon has been given to you to cut down thoughts of fear and any spiritual opposition? What is the prerequisite to activating it and how is it used?

PRINCIPLE 9

DEVELOP FAITH IN THE WAITING – THAT'S ON YOU

Sometimes God will make you wait—that's on Him. But what you do and how you live while you're waiting is on *you*. So much can happen in a season of waiting. Much of this is determined by you. We must be careful that "waiting on God" doesn't cause us to become spiritually complacent. I've seen people make spiritual progress while waiting on God. On the other hand, I've seen people regress spiritually while waiting on God. I can tell you this: Doing nothing while you wait on God is not an option.

What does the Bible say about the topic? What makes the difference? Let me give you just a few answers to these questions.

Focus on God

You must keep your *focus on God*. Proverbs 3:6 *"In all your ways acknowledge Him..."* Many people get this twisted, focusing on the thing they are waiting on, and God is their back up plan. If you find this to be you, don't fret—you are not alone. The "while you wait" principle has made an appearance in this book because waiting is difficult.

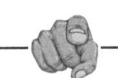

GOD IS YOUR TRUE NORTH, AND STAYING IN HIS PRESENCE ALLOWS YOU TO CONTINUE MOVING IN HIS DIRECTION.

Just remember, in all seasons, even in the waiting, you must keep God as the centerpiece of your life. God is your true north, and staying in His presence allows you to continue moving in His direction. Nothing you are waiting on could ever measure up to being in the presence of God. Your future spouse doesn't measure up to God; your future job doesn't measure up to God; your healing doesn't measure up to God; your breakthrough doesn't measure up to God. NOTHING this world has to offer will ever measure up to God!

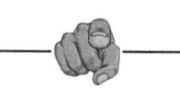

"KEEP THE MAIN THING, THE MAIN THING." FOR A BORN-AGAIN BELIEVER, GOD SHOULD ALWAYS BE THE MAIN THING.

Staying in the presence of God is the main thing to remember while you're waiting. I always tell people who are waiting on God to move in their life, to "Keep the main thing, the main thing." For a born-again believer, God should *always* be the main thing. And the people around them should be able to see that.

Let me explain it another way: Take Ford Automotive, for example. What do you think of when you think of Ford? I bet many of you thought of the F-150 pick-up truck. Not that Ford doesn't make other vehicles, but the F-150 is their bread and butter. That is their "main thing." It helps establish their identity and who they are. The same goes for you spiritually. Keep God as the main thing while you wait, and He will continue to establish your identity—who you are in Him!

Be Intentional in Spending Time with God

While you wait, double down on how much *intentional time* you spend in the presence of God. I used the term "intentional," because this is time that you specifically carve out of your day to be with Him. Maybe your time is early morning, like mine, or maybe it's your lunch hour or bedtime. Find a time in your day to enter the holy presence of God. It should be intimate time, when it's just you and Him. It surprises me how many people don't realize the importance of daily intimacy with God. When I teach on the topic of prayer, I always say that intimacy is one of the pillars of a powerful prayer life. When I am intimate with God, I experience His peace. I enter His presence with thanksgiving and praise.

The Apostle Paul wrote, *"The peace of God, surpasses all understanding..."* (*Philippians 4:7*). That word "surpasses" means superior, greater than, exceeds, outdo, eclipse, or overshadow. In seasons of waiting when I enter His presence by way of intimate prayer, I experience the peace of God that overshadows the waiting. It seems that God shows up in my waiting and produces peace that exceeds the struggle of the wait. Be intentional with your time; give it to God and He will bless it.

Exercise Your Faith

You must also learn to *exercise your faith*. That word "exercise" means to exert, make use of, practice, or apply. Apply your faith through the reading of His word, because the word of God will give you strength in the waiting. One scripture that comes to mind when I think about exercising faith is Romans 8:28: *And we know that in all things God works for the good of those who love him.* This scripture encourages me in the fact that I know God is also working on my behalf. Even when you can't see him working, or when you can't feel Him working, He *is working* all the same. When things don't go your way, God is still working for your good. When you don't get the promotion, God is still working for your good. When you are treated unfairly, God is still working for your good.

Is God Waiting on *You?*

HAVE YOU EVER GIVEN IT ANY THOUGHT THAT MAYBE GOD IS WAITING ON YOU?

I'll give you one more perspective on waiting on God. Have you ever given it any thought that maybe God is waiting on *you?* Maybe God is waiting for you to take the next step, take that leap of faith, or make that tough decision. Ask yourself the question, is God waiting on me? Maybe something in you needs to change before God decides to move. Maybe God is waiting on you to take a step, so He can direct it. Maybe God is waiting for you to take a leap of faith before He shows up in your season of waiting.

Make this a matter of prayer if you need to. Maybe you are reading this and feel like you have waited too long, and you've wasted an opportunity in the waiting. Remember, how we measure time is not how God measures time. God's time is eternal. Our time is counted on a calendar or clock. It is never too late for God to respond and bring that thing to life that you've been waiting for.

I learned a long time ago that He is a God of divine acceleration. What I mean by this is that God can make something happen in a matter of days that should take weeks, and He can make things happen in a matter of weeks that should take years. The bottom-line here is that you trust and obey. Trusting and obeying God will cover both sides of the equation, whether God is waiting on you or you are waiting on God.

God's Timing is Always Right

Let me give you a personal story about waiting on God. As I've mentioned a time or two in this book, when I was around 19 or 20, I was really trying to turn my life around and live wholeheartedly for God. At that age, I had my checklist of things I wanted in life: a godly wife, a family, an education, a career, and some nice things in life to show for it. (In case you're wondering, I would probably rearrange and add to that list at my age now.)

I can remember one of the most influential men of God in my life, Pastor Sam Luke. He'd challenged our church to participate in three days of prayer and fasting. I thought to myself, "Maybe I'll try this prayer and fasting stuff." Nothing else in my life seemed to be providing any joy or meaningful progress towards my dreams. Let me tell you, those three days of prayer and fasting changed the trajectory of my life! Over the next couple of years, my relationship with God strengthened at an extremely fast rate. I couldn't get enough of God and still can't to be honest. My focus was on Him and Him alone. That checklist I mentioned of things I wanted in life was NOTHING compared to my new desire to please God in all my ways. However, I was still waiting and believing that God would provide for me the desires of my heart. The difference now was that my heart totally belonged to God, and I was leaving the rest up to Him and His timing.

I LEARNED A LONG TIME AGO THAT HE IS A GOD OF DIVINE ACCELERATION. WHAT I MEAN BY THIS IS THAT GOD CAN MAKE SOMETHING HAPPEN IN A MATTER OF DAYS THAT SHOULD TAKE WEEKS; HE CAN MAKE THINGS HAPPEN IN A MATTER OF WEEKS THAT SHOULD TAKE YEARS.

Let me fast forward about 18 months to June of 1996. I was attending old-fashioned "camp meeting," which is like summer revival, in case you were wondering. That was the week my life changed forever. On the very first night of that camp meeting, what I was waiting on showed up on the other side of that large sanctuary. This was the night that Jennifer McPherson (now Fussnecker) caught my eye in a way she hadn't before. I didn't fully know then that she was the answer to my waiting. But I know now that God was responding to my unwavering focus on Him in that season. It's now been 28 years ago, and God has continued to bless me in His timing. Too many blessings to count!

What you do while you're waiting on God – *That's on You!* God providing for you in His timing – *That's on Him!*

Applying This Principle–That's on You!

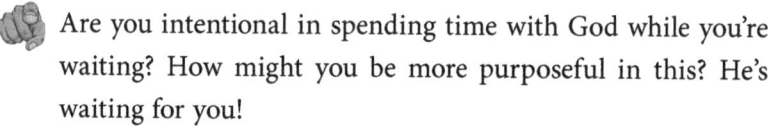 Are you intentional in spending time with God while you're waiting? How might you be more purposeful in this? He's waiting for you!

Have you ever given it thought that God is waiting on *you* before your answer comes? Ask Him if there's something He needs from you first.

Perhaps He's already told you what you need to do (or hear, or say, or give) so that the substance of your faith and obedience is made evident. Look back to the last thing He said to you— did you follow through? You can be sure that when you do, *He will do His part!*

PRINCIPLE 10
PUT YOUR HOPE IN GOD – THAT'S ON YOU

Hope cannot be overstated! In fact, I could argue that hope in God is everything. Pause and think for a moment about hope. Your entire future is attached to something or someone you have put your hope in. Hope acts as an anchor when the storms of life are tossing you amid the waves of the ocean. No matter how bad the storm and

HOPE ACTS AS AN ANCHOR WHEN THE STORMS OF LIFE ARE TOSSING YOU AMID THE WAVES OF THE OCEAN.

how big the waves may be, there is always hope for a better tomorrow.

As a young child I can still remember my dad saying, "Oh, what a difference a day can make." Romans 12:12 tells us to "rejoice in hope." Even when life is dealing you a bad hand in a difficult season, you can still "rejoice in the hope" that this too shall pass. God's desire is to fulfill the plans of Jeremiah 29:11 in your life, *plans to prosper you and not to harm you, plans to give you hope and a future.* Part of God's plan for you is to give you hope.

We Have Eternal Hope

Years ago, I was posed a question. I can't recall if I read the question or if the question was asked directly asked of me, but it's stuck with me nevertheless. The question was, "If you knew for certain that tomorrow would not come, what things would you change?" As I pondered, I thought to myself, "I guess I would tell as many people as I could about the hope they have in Jesus. I would tell them, that although tomorrow will not come on the earth, they have hope in Jesus and can experience His salvation and eternity in heaven."

Even as I'm writing this, it's hitting a little differently. I'm thankful for the hope we have for tomorrow; it motivates me to do much more. Hope in God motivates me to work hard at fulfilling the call of God on my life. It motivates me to be a better husband, a better father, a better pastor, a better friend, etc. Even when I feel like I have failed at these things, I still have hope that God will provide a way for me to succeed in these things in time.

HOPE ALLOWS US TO HIT THE RESET BUTTON AND TRY AGAIN WHEN WE FAIL.

Hope allows us to hit the reset button and try again when we fail. I see people time and time again do this in reverse. They put their hope in the things of the world first, and secondly invite God to come along. Then, when things don't go well, they ask God to fix it. If this is you, then you should think about making a shift in the way you prioritize hope. Put your hope in God first, and then let everything else fall into place. If I were preaching right now, I would tell the congregation, "Somebody shout EVERYTHING!" Yeah, it's ok to shout "EVERYTHING" to yourself right now—no one is looking.

There is nothing like hoping in the Lord. Over the years, I have learned this to be true. To be honest, I have put my hope in some things and some people and regretted it. I have learned the hard way that things are temporary, and people are human. Both things and people are subject to worldly influence and fallibility. Ultimately, we must put our hope in the Lord. Our hope for ALL things must be put in the Lord! This includes the hope we have for our goals and dreams in life: family, children, career goals, relationships, calling in ministry, and so much more.

Hope in the Lord Brings Renewed Strength

The verse of scripture referenced in this *THAT'S ON YOU!* nugget comes from the prophet Isaiah. He explains what occurs when we put our hope in the Lord.

> *Even youths grow tired and weary, and young men stumble and fall, but those who hope in the Lord will renew their strength. They will soar on wings like eagles; they will run and not grow weary, they will walk and not be faint. (Isaiah 40:31)*

That is powerful scripture to say the least. There are some powerful action words in this scripture that I believe are worthy of spending a little time on. The words renew, soar, run, and walk are all words that indicate progress on your Christian journey. This simple observation is refreshing to me, because most of the super-saints that I know seem to live like this 24/7 and frankly, I know many of us don't always feel this way! Are you asking yourself right now, what is a super-saint? You know, every church has at least one super-saint, lol. Do I have to describe them specifically? Ok, now that we all have that one person in our minds, let's move along, shall we? Let's get back to Isaiah 40:31.

1) "Renew" means to restore something to its original state. Dude! I feel like I need to be renewed every day. Now that I'm thinking, I am *sure* I do! Thankfully, the Bible says that God's mercies are new every day! So, if I need renewing every morning, God's mercy makes that possible.

2) "Soar" means to maintain elevation with little to no energy exertion. Well then, that'll preach! Evaluate the things in your life that you are exerting entirely too much energy into, and you still seem to be losing ground. This scripture says if you put your hope in the Lord, you will maintain

IF YOU PUT YOUR HOPE IN THE LORD, YOU WILL MAINTAIN AND INCREASE YOUR LEVEL OF PROFICIENCY, WITH LITTLE TO NO ENERGY!

and increase your level of proficiency, with little to no energy! Wait what? Read that again, before you move on: "WITH LITTLE TO NO ENERGY!" Yes, when you hope in the Lord, you soar on wings like eagles with little to no energy!

As a bi-vocational pastor, I am often asked the question, "Pastor, how do you have the time to do all the things you do?" My only answer is to say that God allows me to soar like an eagle when I put my hope in him. Is it just me right now or is someone else singing the lyrics, "Fly like an eagle, into the sea; I want to fly like an eagle, let the Spirit carry me." If you know, you know!

3) "Run" means to move at a pace faster than a walk. One definition of run that I read describes running as "to never have both or all feet on the ground at the same time." Wouldn't it be great to pursue your dreams and goals in this way? Well, if you put your hope in the Lord, this verse says you can! I know some pastors like this. They never seem to have both feet on the ground at once. I would say, without hoping in the Lord, it's nearly impossible to live like this for any substantial amount of time.

4) "Walk" means to move forward, never having both feet off the ground at once. Basically, this is the opposite of run, but still making progress. So, it is ok to walk. Not sure if you needed to hear that like I did, but I will say it again: "It's ok to walk." In fact, I have learned that you almost always must learn to walk before you can run.

Put your hope in the Lord – THAT'S ON YOU! And in the hoping, know that He will renew you, and give you power to walk, run, and soar — THAT'S ON HIM!

Applying This Principle—That's on You!

 Read the following verses and identify the function of hope in the storms of life. Where and to what is the hope secured?

We who have fled [to Him] for refuge would have strong encouragement and indwelling strength to hold tightly to the hope set before us. This hope [this confident assurance] we have as an anchor of the soul [it cannot slip and it cannot break down under whatever pressure bears upon it] — a safe and steadfast hope that enters within the veil [of the heavenly temple, that most Holy Place in which the very presence of God dwells] (Hebrews 6:18b-19 AMP)

 Reread Isaiah 40:31 referenced in this chapter. It says that those who hope in the Lord will have renewed strength. This word "hope" is the Hebrew word *qavah*. From *Strong's Lexicon:*

"To wait, to look for, to hope, to expect, meaning to bind together by twisting... This waiting is not passive but involves a confident expectation of God's intervention or fulfillment of His promises. The term can also imply a sense of gathering or binding together, as in the intertwining of strands to form a cord, symbolizing strength and unity."

How does understanding of this word increase your sense of hope in the tension or stretch of waiting? To whom is your soul bound together?

 In light of the Hebrew context, how is your strength renewed? How does this hope empower you to walk, run and soar? Now waiting in hope doesn't seem so bad, does it?!

DEPEND ON GOD – THAT'S ON YOU

You may not be familiar with the story of the three Hebrew boys that we find in chapter 3 of the Book of Daniel. A quick synopsis of the story is that the majority of the Jewish people had been taken captive to the land of Babylon, where King Nebuchadnezzar was ruler. His command for everyone living in Babylon was to bow down in worship to a statue made in his image. The Hebrews were aware of Scripture and the commands of God: 1. You shall have no other gods before Me. 2. You shall not make or worship graven images. These were God's commandments taught since the beginning of Israel's covenant with Yahweh. They were so important that He engraved them in stone tablets for His people to live by.

You Can Depend on God with Your Life

These three young men, Shadrach, Meshach and Abednego, had a choice to make: bow down to the image of Kind Nebuchadnezzar or be thrown into a fiery furnace. They chose the fiery furnace. The outcome was miraculous to say the least! Not only did they survive the fiery furnace, but Nebuchadnezzar exclaimed, "Look! I see four men walking around in the fire, unbound and unharmed, and the fourth looks like a son of the gods."

The king didn't know Him, but He saw that these faithful Hebrews had been joined by the Son of the living God in the furnace. God not only protected them, but He used them to influence King

Nebuchadnezzar. When the king saw this miraculous rescue right in front of his eyes, he said,

> *Praise be to the God of Shadrach, Meshach and Abednego, who has sent his angel and rescued his servants! They trusted in Him and defied the king's command and were willing to give up their lives rather than serve or worship any god except their own God. Therefore I decree that the people of any nation or language who say anything against the God of Shadrach, Meshach and Abednego be cut into pieces and their houses be turned into piles of rubble, for no other god can save in this way. Then the king promoted Shadrach, Meshach and Abednego in the province of Babylon. (Daniel 3:28-30)*

WHEN THE THREE HEBREW BOYS STOOD THEIR GROUND AND HONORED GOD, THEY ACTIVATED THE POWER OF GOD!

This is one of the greatest *That's on You* stories ever told! They literally depended on God with their lives. Only God could have performed this miracle, but He needed a willing person who would trust Him to provide deliverance. When the three Hebrew boys stood their ground and honored God, they activated the power of God in their personal lives. In other words, the power of God already existed since the beginning of time, but their dependence on God is what activated it.

Depending on God Activates the Impossible

I can remember like it was yesterday a "fiery furnace" circumstance that Jennifer and I found ourselves in. I want to share it with you. We were expecting our third child, Madilyn, in the fall of 2004. One day while I was at work, somewhere around midday I received a call from Jennifer. I could hear the distress in her voice, and it was evident that she was struggling. She said, "Scott, I just got a call from the doctor, and I need you to come home."

Immediate panic and a heart-sinking feeling came over me. It was very unusual for her to ask me to leave work and come home. Of course, I asked her what was wrong. She told me that bloodwork results had come back and were showing that our baby would be born with severe disabilities. I hustled home to be with her. When I got home, she was sitting on the steps and the phone was next to her. I could tell she hadn't moved, and was still sitting in the same place as when she'd called me thirty minutes before. She began to explain more of the report of which the doctor had informed her.

The doctor had mentioned something called Trisomy 18 but wanted to schedule an appointment to talk about things in person. We did some research and were disheartened. We found that babies with Trisomy 18 will often not make it through birth, and if they do make it, they will generally have life-threatening birth defects and very short life expectancy. We were scared, we were questioning God, and our faith was being tested.

Within a week or so we met with the doctor, and he confirmed what we'd read about this disability. I can't remember any of the exact words from the conversation with the doctor that day. However, I can remember the general conversation and how Jennifer and I responded. Sometime after we were given the medical definition of what we were up against, the doctor asked us, "Do you really know the difficulties of trying to raise a baby with Trisomy 18?" I asked the doctor, "What do you mean?" He responded, "Well, you still have time to consider other options."

After asking some clarifying questions, Jennifer and I realized he was asking us to consider aborting our baby. The Spirit of God emboldened us, and we told him that was not an option because of our faith. We left the doctor's office that day and never saw him again.

When preaching, I tell this story from time to time; I like to say, "We fired that doctor on that day. The doctor worked for us, and we had choices of who we wanted to pay for our medical services."

So, our next step was to find a doctor we felt more comfortable working with. Jennifer called the doctor who delivered our first daughter, Claudia. We trusted him and valued his opinion about what we were up against. He immediately scheduled an appointment for her to have additional bloodwork done. The news we got this time was better and he gave us some confidence that our baby was going to be fine.

Nevertheless, in the back of our minds, we were still afraid, and we were still questioning God about all that was happening. I wanted to hold a healthy baby in my arms to erase all doubt. At that time in my life I knew that God could do anything. But I couldn't totally erase the thought in mind, "What if the first doctor was right?" This reminds me of the father who came to Jesus for his son's healing and said,: *"I believe; help me with my unbelief"* (Mark 9:24). I was experiencing belief and doubt simultaneously.

So, the day finally came on January 19, 2005, when our baby was born. In honesty, I was in the birthing room still waiting for confirmation that our baby was ok. I hollered over to the doctor, "Is she ok, doc?" He responded, "She looks good."

That was not good enough for me, so I repeated, "No doc, I mean does she look ok?" And he said "Dad, she is a healthy baby girl!" I was doing the Holy Ghost two-step in my mind! God did it again! Looking back now, I can see this was one of the ways that God was "helping my unbelief."

I could never tell this story without throwing in our inside family joke that Maddie has grown to be a perfect unicorn. LOL, if you know, you know! I love my tribe; family means so much to me!

THE NEXT TIME YOU ARE FACED WITH A FIERY FURNACE DECISION, REMEMBER THAT NOTHING IS IMPOSSIBLE FOR GOD!

Depending on God is not always going be easy when you're up against a fiery furnace—many times it means life or death! The next time you are faced with a fiery furnace decision, remember that nothing is impossible for God— *THAT'S ON HIM!* Depend on God for the impossible—*THAT'S ON YOU!*

Applying This Principle–That's on You!

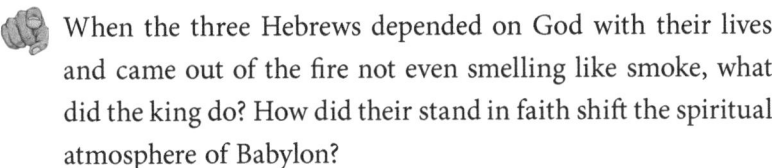

When the three Hebrews depended on God with their lives and came out of the fire not even smelling like smoke, what did the king do? How did their stand in faith shift the spiritual atmosphere of Babylon?

Think back on a time when you faced a fiery trial, perhaps even a life-threatening one. Did you depend on God? Did you find the Son of the living God walking with you? How did He reveal that He was with you?

Read Daniel 3:28-30 found at the beginning of this chapter. How did their experience and trust in God affect their personal positions and influence?

Read Daniel chapter 2. How did Daniel's trust in God when facing death launch his enduring spiritual legacy, without which we wouldn't even have a record of these events? Neither would the wise men, the Eastern magi king-makers, have known about the Star of Bethlehem and come to crown the Infant Jesus as King (Matthew 2:1-11)! Depending on God is *always* worth it!

PRINCIPLE 12

MANAGE THE POWER IN YOUR WORDS – THAT'S ON YOU

Where do I even begin with the topic of managing the power of the tongue? As I've grown older, I've come to realize the power of the words we speak. Simple words can build us up and yet, they can also hurt so badly. There have been so many times in life that I wished I could take something back that I'd said. Always remember before you speak, that you can't "unsay" something.

As I recollect those who have influenced me positively over the years, I realize much of their influence came by way of the encouraging words they spoke into my life. I'm not sure of the exact science of the brain's response when we receive praise, but I do know it makes you feel good! I've even heard that the brain's response to praise is the same as if we'd received a monetary reward. Never underestimate the power of telling someone "good job" or "well done!" I can remember when I was a child, my parents always believed in me. They would be sure to build me up when I did things well. That's not to say they didn't reinforce the expectations around the house when I needed some correction!

Our Words have Spiritual Consequences

As a pastor, I've been able to clearly see the spiritual ramifications of what I say and how my words impact many things and many people.

BEING ABLE TO CONTROL WHAT WE SAY AND WHAT WE DON'T SAY MAKES A SIGNIFICANT IMPACT ON OUR WORK RELATED TO THE KINGDOM OF GOD.

Being able to control what we say and what we *don't* say makes a significant impact on our work related to the Kingdom of God. The enemy does not want us to discover the power of what comes out of our mouths. This is because he knows that in our words, we have the power to speak life!

The tongue has the power of life and death... (Proverbs 18:21)

I want to continue to unpack the power of the words we say, in hopes of making it practical for you. The Book of James really hits hard on the topic of the tongue and the words we speak. James talks about how such a small part of the human body, the tongue, can have such a lasting impact.

When we put bits into the mouths of horses to make them obey us, we can turn the whole animal. Or take ships as an example. Although they are so large and are driven by strong winds, they are steered by a very small rudder wherever the pilot wants to go. Likewise, the tongue is a small part of the body, but it makes great boasts. Consider what a great forest is set on fire by a small spark. The tongue also is a fire, a world of evil among the parts of the body. It corrupts the whole body, sets the whole course of one's life on fire, and is itself set on fire by hell. (James 3:3-6)

The words we say are not just meaningless syllables that come out of our mouths. It's important to understand that our heart is the driving force of all we say and do. The truth is, our words are an outward reflection of an inward thought or idea. Spiritually speaking, the heart is the production factory of the words we say. Not only does the heart produce the good things we say, the heart also produces the bad.

Then Jesus turned to the crowd and said, "Come, listen and open your heart to understand. What truly contaminates a person is not what he puts into his mouth but what comes out of his mouth. That's what makes people defiled." (Matthew 15:10-11 TPT)

For example, the heart produces praise and worship unto God as we sing songs. However, that same heart can produce slander and gossip with our words. I can't tell you how many times I've attended great church services with folks who were praising the Lord with all their might, only to go have lunch afterwards with those same people, and they gossip about their church family. Pro Tip: Don't be that person! Rather, pay attention to the plank in your own eye.

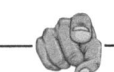

THE HEART IS THE PRODUCTION FACTORY OF THE WORDS WE SAY. NOT ONLY DOES THE HEART PRODUCE THE GOOD THINGS WE SAY, THE HEART ALSO PRODUCES THE BAD.

What comes out of your mouth is indicative of the wickedness of the heart.

But the tongue is not able to be tamed. It's a fickle, unrestrained evil that spews out words full of toxic poison! We use our tongue to praise God our Father and then turn around and curse a person who was made in his very image! Out of the same mouth we pour out words of praise one minute and curses the next. My brothers and sisters, this should never be!

Would you look for olives hanging on a fig tree or go to pick figs from a grapevine? Is it possible that fresh and bitter water can flow out of the same spring? So neither can a bitter spring produce fresh water. (James 3:8-12 TPT)

What Comes from our Mouths is Indicative of Our Hearts

IF THE HEART IS IN THE RIGHT CONDITION, IT'S CAPABLE OF SPEAKING WORDS OF LIFE. THIS IS THE ONLY WAY FOR YOU TO STAND A CHANCE AT CONSISTENTLY MANAGING YOUR TONGUE.

In Matthew 15:18, Jesus said, *"But the things that come out of a person's mouth come from the heart...."* His words confirm the imperative that your heart *MUST* be regenerated. The word "regenerated" simply means to be spiritually renewed, or made new. A synonym for regeneration is the new birth, or "born again" experience. A heart must be given new birth, or be born again of the Spirit, to produce anything that is truly good. I sometimes say that a regenerated heart is like receiving a spiritual heart transplant. If the heart is in the right condition, it's capable of speaking words of life. This is the only way for you to stand a chance at consistently managing your tongue. When you manage your tongue well, you can more effectively reflect the image of Christ.

Referring again to the Book of James 1:19, he tells us, *"Everyone should be quick to listen and slow to speak."* Spiritually speaking, we sometimes learn best when we say nothing! This leaves room for you to allow God to speak into your life. Being slow to speak allows you to obey what Scripture says about the tongue:

> *Those who consider themselves religious and yet do not keep a tight rein (bridle) on their tongues deceive themselves, and their religion is worthless. (James 1:26)*

While studying for one of my sermons a few years back, I heard a preacher say, "Sometimes it would be better for people to think you're a fool, than to open your mouth and leave no doubt." In Proverbs 10:19

we also read, *In the multitude of words, sin is not lacking, but he who RESTRAINS his lips is wise* (NKJV). In the book of Scott Fussnecker it says, "You have two ears and one mouth for a reason: Talk half and listen double."

"SOMETIMES IT WOULD BE BETTER FOR PEOPLE TO THINK YOU'RE A FOOL, THAN TO OPEN YOUR MOUTH AND LEAVE NO DOUBT."

Our Words Influence Our Witness for Christ

I want to share a story about my personal journey to manage my tongue. Somewhere around the age of nineteen or twenty, I began to get serious about trying to live a life fully devoted to God. During this time, I had difficulty controlling my mouth. My language could be a bit colorful to say the least. At the time, I was attending Northern Kentucky University and working part-time at a furniture warehouse. Part of my job responsibility was to assemble tables scheduled to be delivered to customers the following day. I really didn't like this part of my job. I would be thinking on my drive to work, "I wonder how many 'bleeping' tables will be waiting for me when I get there?" Sometimes it would be 25 or 30 tables, and when I would take my first glance from the opposite end of the warehouse upon arrival, I had a few choice words for those tables. LOL!

On a more serious note, I started to make this a spiritual matter. I would get out my utility knife and tools and say "OK, no cussing today." Even as I am writing this, I am chuckling at the thought of it. As trivial as it may sound now, at the time it was stunting my spiritual development. I would finish putting tables together on some days and think, "Not bad, only four cuss words today." Then I had to pray this big prayer to be forgiven and feel bad for the rest of my work shift for the things I said to those poor tables. You see, once I started to make a better effort to live for God, that type of language just didn't feel right coming out of my mouth. Even worse, if this kind of thing happened in front of other people, it negatively influenced my ability to be a witness to them.

In time, God continued to give me the strength to control what comes out of my mouth. Not to say that I sometimes don't need to pray over that thought bubble over my head when I want to mouth off. Yes, pastor's struggle with this as well, in case you were wondering! That is when I remember what 2 Corinthians 10:5 tells me to do and I *"...take that thought captive and make it obedient to Christ!"*

Spiritual Tools to Manage Our Tongues

One practical way to make every thought obedient to Christ is to activate Psalm 34:1 in your life: *"His praise shall continually be in my mouth."* "Continually" means that something is repeated frequently in the same way, or without interruption, constantly. Leave no room for negative talk. In the good times, thank God that He has provided a way for you. Thank God in the bad times, that there's an opportunity for a miracle. Thank God on the mountaintop for His goodness and provision. Thank God in the valley, that there's an opportunity for Him to bring you out.

GET RID OF THAT OLD "STINKIN' THINKIN'" FROM THE OLD YOU, BEFORE YOU GAVE YOUR HEART TO CHRIST.

A second practical way to make every thought obedient to Christ is to activate Philippians 4:8 in your life: *Brothers and sisters, whatever is true, whatever is noble, whatever is right, whatever is pure, whatever is lovely, whatever is admirable—if anything is excellent or praiseworthy—think about such things.* In other words, get rid of that old "stinkin' thinkin'" from the old you, before you gave your heart to Christ.

These two practical ways are spiritual tools of warfare that we use to overcome our fallen nature or any enemy. Remember, this warfare that I speak of is not physical warfare, rather it is spiritual warfare. Ephesians 6:12 says, *For our struggle is not against flesh and blood, but against the rulers, against the authorities, against the powers of this dark world and against the spiritual forces of evil in the heavenly realms.*

I frequently tell people who seek advice from me regarding this kind of warfare, "You can't use physical weapons in a spiritual battle." You must use spiritual weapons, to win spiritual warfare. There are many spiritual tools provided for you: prayer, praise, faith, reading and speaking the word, renewing your mind, meditating on God, reading daily devotionals, etc. Continue to build your arsenal against the "old man" and

CONTINUE TO BUILD YOUR ARSENAL AGAINST THE "OLD MAN" AND THE ENEMY, WHO ARE ALWAYS WORKING IN OPPOSITION TO YOUR NEW NATURE.

the enemy, who are always working in opposition to your new nature.

The Apostle Paul wrote about this struggle with the old man in his letter to the Romans. He finally came to the conclusion that you must simply reckon it dead and your new nature alive in Christ. Read his words on how the old, fallen nature is overcome, so that our tongue and its potential for fiery trouble can be tamed:

> *I am a human being made of flesh and trafficked as a slave under sin's authority. I'm a mystery to myself, for I want to do what is right, but end up doing what my moral instincts condemn....And now I realize that it is no longer my true self doing it, but the unwelcome intruder of sin in my humanity....*
>
> *Truly, deep within my true identity, I love to do what pleases God. But I discern another power operating in my humanity, waging a war against the moral principles of my conscience and*

bringing me into captivity as a prisoner to the "law" of sin—this unwelcome intruder in my humanity. What an agonizing situation I am in! So who has the power to rescue this miserable man from the unwelcome intruder of sin and death? I give all my thanks to God, for his mighty power has finally provided a way out through our Lord Jesus, the Anointed One! So if left to myself, the flesh is aligned with the law of sin, but now my renewed mind is fixed on and submitted to God's righteous principles.

So now the case is closed. There remains no accusing voice of condemnation against those who are joined in life-union with Jesus, the Anointed One. For the "law" of the Spirit of life flowing through the anointing of Jesus has liberated us from the "law" of sin and death. So now every righteous requirement of the law can be fulfilled through the Anointed One living his life in us. And we are free to live, not according to our flesh, but by the dynamic power of the Holy Spirit! (Romans 7:14b-8:4 TPT)

I'm believing in Jesus' name, that God will help you, just like he helped me. I know you can overcome and learn to manage the power of the tongue. When you fail at it and you sometimes will, God will always be there to pick you up to start again.

He's given us all we need to live the overcoming life by the power of the Holy Spirit within us. Using spiritual tools to renew your mind and fix them on His principles to live in life-union with Jesus—*THAT'S ON YOU!* Providing the grace to manage the power in your tongue for Kingdom purposes—*THAT'S ON HIM!*

Applying This Principle—That's on You!

 Reread James 3:3-6. Note that he refers to whole large animals, large ships, strong winds, great forest fires. How does this relate to great boasts from our tongue? How is the tongue a fire and what are its results?

 What is the source, or production factory, of our words? How are they indicators of our spiritual condition?

 Reread the passage James 3:8-12 in this chapter. What does he mean that you can't pick figs from a grapevine, neither can both fresh and bitter water flow from the same spring? How does this relate to your words and the condition of your heart?

 The only way to tame the tongue is to regenerate the heart by being born again and by renewal of the mind. Consider the wisdom found in Proverbs 4:23: *Above all else, guard your heart, for everything you do [or issues of life] flows from it.* How does this verse parallel the wisdom found in the Book of James?

 Read again the passage from Romans 7:14b-8:4. Note that "this body of death" in verse 24 is a reference to the Roman punishment of chaining a dead body to a criminal. As the "body of death" decayed, its putrefaction infected him, causing the criminal's death. What a picture of the old man and its corruption, which leads to spiritual death! What is the only way you can be free from the "old man," this body of death, who wants to use your tongue in speaking deadly words?

PRINCIPLE 13
DIE TO SELF
– THAT'S ON YOU

For what will it profit a man if he gains the whole world and forfeits his soul? Or what shall a man give in return for his soul. (Matthew 16:26)

I've probably seen and heard this scripture quoted hundreds of times over the years. It seems that everyone who has heard or read this verse believes it to be true. However, not everyone who reads or hears it lives the kind of life that reflects his or her beliefs about the verse.

Maybe you're reading this, and you're not sure what this verse means; I'll try to help with that. At Foundation, where I pastor, we talk a lot about the 3 T's: Time, Talent, and Treasure. We ask ourselves, "How do I use my time for God; how do I use my talent for God; and how do I steward my finances in a way that pleases God?"

Invest Your 3Ts in the Kingdom for Eternal Dividends

I have found that some people spend an enormous amount of their time, talent, and treasure building their life around things that have nothing to do with God. This is often a reflection of their walk with God. Let me be clear, there is nothing wrong with devoting some of your 3Ts to things that do not nurture the soul, or your inner, spiritual being. The question then becomes, "What really needs to be nurtured most in your life? The soul or your life outside of the soul?"

A SOUL FIRST NURTURED BY GOD WILL NEVER WRONGLY INFORM THE FLESH.

For me personally, the answer is clear: I will nurture my soul first, so that my soul can nurture the other parts of my life. I must be careful in my own life that I do not get this backwards. It must be in the correct order: 1. I must nurture the soul with the things of God first. 2. Everything else comes after that. A soul first nurtured by God will never wrongly inform the flesh.

"Why would you say, 'What will we eat?' or 'What will we drink?' or 'What will we wear?' For that is what the unbelievers chase after. Doesn't your heavenly Father already know the things your bodies require?

"So above all, constantly seek God's kingdom and his righteousness, then all these less important things will be given to you abundantly. (Matthew 6:31b-33 TPT)

The question posed here from the Book of Matthew can be framed to ask, "But what if you gained the whole world; would that be worth it?" If you gained the whole world, would you need anything else?

Let's look a little deeper. First, we as humanity are incapable of gaining the whole world. Jesus' wisdom in this question is so deep and profound! Jesus fully knows that no one can gain the whole world, yet he still asked the question "But what if?" What if you could? What if you could gain the whole world? Would it be worth your soul then?

EVERY DAY PEOPLE FORFEIT THEIR SOUL FOR A WHOLE LOT LESS THAN THE "WHOLE WORLD."

I find it quite interesting that every day people forfeit their soul for much less than the "whole world." So many people spend their lifetime neglecting, in essence forfeiting, their soul to chase things that really don't matter when viewed through the lens of eternity.

Deny the Old Life to Find the True Life

Jesus taught His disciples this principle, exhorting them to deny themselves and live the crucified life. In other words, if we spend our lives without eternity in view, even what we think we have will be lost:

Then he said to them all: "Whoever wants to be my disciple must deny themselves and take up their cross and follow me. (Luke 9:23)

[A]nd anyone who does not take up his cross and follow Me is not worthy of Me. (Matthew 10:38)

"Let me make this clear: A single grain of wheat will never be more than a single grain of wheat unless it drops into the ground and dies. Because then it sprouts and produces a great harvest of wheat—all because one grain died.

"The person who loves his life and pampers himself will miss true life! But the one who detaches his life from this world and abandons himself to me, will find true life and enjoy it forever! (John 12:24-26 TPT)

The Apostle Paul carried forward this principle in his letters to Timothy and the churches:

Here is a trustworthy saying: If we died with him, we will also live with him; if we endure, we will also reign with him. (2 Timothy 2:11-12)

I have been crucified with Christ and I no longer live, but Christ lives in me. (Galatians 2:20)

IF WE DIE TO SELF AND THE LESSER THINGS OF THIS WORLD, WE'LL GAIN THINGS OF SO MUCH MORE VALUE—CHRIST WILL LIVE IN US AND WE WILL REIGN WITH HIM FOREVER!

Said another way, if we die to self and the lesser things of this world, we'll gain things of so much more value—Christ will live in us and we will reign with Him forever!

Over the years there have been many things I could have gained that would have been of worldly value, but of no value to feed my soul and prepare me for eternity. I must admit that I haven't been perfect at this, but I've learned and continue to grow. Nurturing the soul takes sacrifice and dying to self—*THAT'S ON YOU!* Christ's power alive and ruling through you—*THAT'S ON HIM!*

Applying This Principle—That's on You!

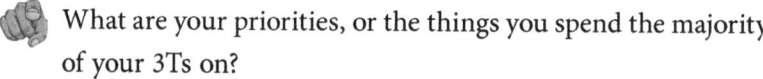 What are your priorities, or the things you spend the majority of your 3Ts on?

Reread Matthew 6:31b-33. How does Jesus refer to those who chase after, food, drink, and clothing? Describe how can all these things be yours without effort, if you wisely invest your 3Ts?

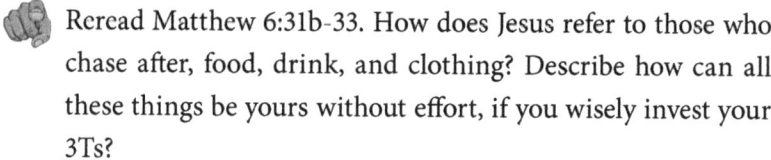 Are you viewing your life with a narrow field of focus or with the lens of eternity?

What does it mean to deny yourself and take up your cross (Luke 9:23)? If you don't do this, how does Jesus consider you (Luke 9:23)?

Read again John 12:24-26. How do we find true life and enjoy it forever? Is there anything you're holding onto that would be an obstacle to that glorious eternity with God?

PRINCIPLE 14

DROP YOUR NETS & FOLLOW JESUS – THAT'S ON YOU

One day as Jesus was standing by the Lake of Gennesaret, the people were crowding around him and listening to the word of God. He saw at the water's edge two boats, left there by the fishermen, who were washing their nets. He got into one of the boats, the one belonging to Simon, and asked him to put out a little from shore. Then he sat down and taught the people from the boat.

When he had finished speaking, he said to Simon, "Put out into deep water, and let down the nets for a catch."

Simon answered, "Master, we've worked hard all night and haven't caught anything. But because you say so, I will let down the nets."

When they had done so, they caught such a large number of fish that their nets began to break. So they signaled their partners in the other boat to come and help them, and they came and filled both boats so full that they began to sink. When Simon Peter saw this, he fell at Jesus' knees and said, "Go away from me, Lord; I am a sinful man!" For he and all his companions were astonished at the catch of fish they had taken, and so were James and John, the sons of Zebedee, Simon's partners.

Then Jesus said to Simon, "Don't be afraid; from now on you will fish for people." So they pulled their boats up on shore, left everything and followed him. (Luke 5:2-11)

Drop your nets, come, and follow me. *That's on you.* When we read about the interaction that Jesus had with Simon and Andrew, it seems so easy to do what they did. I am here to tell you that dropping your nets is not always easy; it is a really big deal. It requires faith and courage. You make a living with your nets; you feed your family with your nets; much about your future has been built around what you accomplish with your nets.

I am not sure what your "nets" are today, but whatever they are, they are of utmost importance to your livelihood and well-being. Your "nets" are very important to you, and something you can't imagine living without. Maybe your nets are your job, maybe your bank account, maybe your home, etc.

Will You Drop Your Nets to Follow Him?

If God asked you to walk away from these to follow Him, would you? I'm not indicating that these nets in your life aren't important,

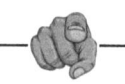

DROPPING YOUR NETS IS ONE THING, BUT FOLLOWING JESUS MAKES DROPPING YOUR NETS WORK OUT IN THE END. THOSE ARE TWO DIFFERENT THINGS.

but I am saying that none of them are more important than the power of God and His favor on your life. Keep in mind that when we read the Bible in the 21st Century, we know what the outcome for Simon and Andrew was. So, this can make dropping your nets seem somewhat easy.

Well, let me ask you this question today, do you have things in life that you are not letting go of that you know you should? I could give you tons of scriptures from the Bible about faith and encourage you to let go like Simon and Andrew did. It's as easy as that, right? Well, we know this isn't the case. Furthermore, Simon and Andrew took a second step beyond dropping their nets. Not only did they drop their nets, but they also followed Jesus. Dropping your nets is one thing, but following Jesus makes dropping your nets work out in the end. Those are two different things.

I have known some people that have had an authentic experience with God, and they "dropped" the thing in their life that they believed was keeping them from God's plan and purpose. However, they didn't follow Him.

Following Jesus Leads to Kingdom Purpose

I have an example in my own life of something that was very hard to let go of. Many people do not know that I began my professional career as a public school teacher and a coach in the fall of 1992. It's all I ever wanted to do. I had a great passion for kids. I still do by the way!

It was around 2004 when God began to deal with me about my time, specifically what I was pouring my time into. I had been a Varsity Head Soccer Coach for 10 years at a large school in Cincinnati by this time. It took a tremendous amount of my time and attention after a full day of teaching—not to mention the added stress that it caused in my life. I was deeply passionate about it!

God began to deal with me about an even deeper call to become a pastor. Man, oh man, I can remember how anxious it made me feel when I would think about it for too long. No one knew about this call on my life for a few years. My dilemma was that I knew I wouldn't be able to continue coaching and fulfill the

MY HEART'S DESIRE AT THAT TIME HAD TRANSITIONED FROM WANTING TO FULFILL MY OWN HOPES AND DREAMS AS A COACH, TO WANTING TO PLEASE GOD ABOVE ALL ELSE!

commitments of pastoring a church. The time commitment would simply be too much. So I thought, "Just don't tell anyone and keep coaching."

After much prayer and consideration, I eventually resigned my coaching position in 2007. This was a very difficult thing for me. But my heart's desire at that time had transitioned from wanting to fulfill my own hopes and dreams as a coach, to wanting to please God above all else!

As time went on this call of God on my life became so overwhelming that I could no longer keep it to myself. My wife was the first person I decided to share the call of being a pastor with; I didn't talk to her about it until somewhere around 2009. I can remember the conversation as if it was yesterday. This was a hard step for me to take because I knew once I verbalized it to someone, it was no longer my own little secret. I thought, if I keep it to myself, no real action is required.

When I told Jennifer, the news didn't go exactly the way I'd initially hoped it would. Her response to me was, "Do you even know what you're saying right now?" You see, she had spent her entire life as a "pastor's kid," and she knew the strain and difficulties of pastoring a church as well as anyone.

As I recall, within about an hour or so, Jennifer stopped me and said, "Scott, I'll support you in whatever you're called to do." This was a huge weight lifted off my shoulders. I knew that I was going to need her full support to live out the calling of God. At that time, we were also serving in ministry at her father's church (Oak Creek Church in Kettering, OH) that she grew up in. This made things even more difficult for us to pursue becoming pastors of our own church.

Step one had been telling Jennifer, and step two was figuring out how to break this news to her family; we were deeply troubled by this. As I've mentioned, family is everything to us. We knew leaving Oak Creek Church would be very difficult, not only for us, but for her family as well. We didn't want to hurt anyone, but we were also trying to be obedient to God.

From time to time, Jennifer and I still recall meeting with her parents for dinner and sharing the news with them that God was calling us to leave Oak Creek to become church planters. We told them, "We have no church members, no church name, no church location, we just have a vision to plant a life-giving church." Thinking about that dinner is a vivid memory. We will be forever thankful that her parents were always supportive of our endeavors, although we knew they were sad to see us go.

I can remember the evening we received a call from Jennifer's dad, Jim, when he was just a few days from going to heaven. It was late at night, and we were not expecting him to call. I could hear him say on the phone, "Jenn, I just want you to know how proud I am of the work you and Scott are doing at Foundation, and I understand." Jim is no longer with us, but he still touches the people we serve at Foundation through his wisdom as a father and mentor. There are times when God is really blessing the people of our church when Jennifer and I look at one another and ask, "What if we'd never answered the call to plant Foundation?"

Foundation Community Church hosted its first weekly service in 2011. This didn't happen overnight; you just don't wake up one day and plant a church. The time that I once poured into building a competitive soccer program was now being used to fulfill this deeper call of

I HAD TO DROP MY NET FIRST! WHEN I DID, GOD MOVED.

God in our lives. But remember that I had to drop my net first! When I did, God moved. Not that God couldn't have moved anyway; however, He was able to see that I had to change my time habits to be a pastor— *THAT WAS ON ME!* Bringing the fish into the net of Foundation and His Kingdom—*THAT'S ON HIM!*

Applying This Principle—That's on You!

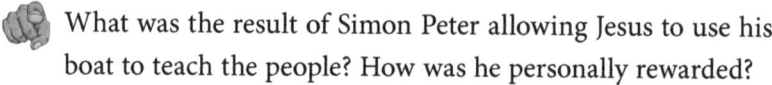 What was the result of Simon Peter allowing Jesus to use his boat to teach the people? How was he personally rewarded?

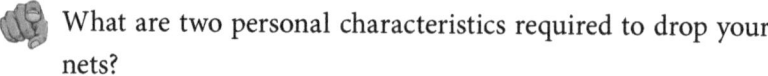 What are two personal characteristics required to drop your nets?

 What do nets represent in your life? Are they being used to advance the Kingdom?

Would you drop them if Jesus asked you to?

What is the next important step that must be taken after dropping your nets?

PRINCIPLE 15
JUST START
– THAT'S ON YOU

Someone stopped me as they were leaving church a few years back. They said, "Pastor, that series *Just Start* you preached really helped me." Of course, I was curious to hear more, so I encouraged her to elaborate. She explained that I'd said you don't have to wait until everything in life is lined up perfectly to begin that thing which God is calling you to do. For her, "that thing" was attending church regularly, and she hadn't missed a Sunday since hearing that *Just Start* message.

Over the years, I've seen so many people not start something because they feel they aren't ready yet. The excuses I've heard are plenty: you don't know my situation; my schedule is so busy; my past is too checkered; I'm not qualified; I'm not good enough, etc. The enemy has a really crafty way of keeping people from getting started on the things God is encouraging them to do. The enemy knows the power of God, and that once you experience that true power, there's no stopping you!

Humility is the Best Starting Point

Let me be honest, you will probably never feel like you are totally prepared or equipped to do great things for God. This is actually a great place of humility to start from. Truth is, it's only by the power of God, working in and through you, that anything great can be accomplished. If you just start, God will equip you to accomplish His work. I usually look back in hindsight and realize it was only by the power of God He's worked through me, equipping me to influence some folks along the way. It seems it's easier to look back and see the power of God than it is to look forward in faith.

TRUTH IS, IT'S ONLY BY THE POWER OF GOD, WORKING IN AND THROUGH YOU, THAT ANYTHING GREAT CAN BE ACCOMPLISHED.

Now may the God peace...equip you with everything good for doing His will and may He work in us what is pleasing to Him. (Hebrews 13:20)

God is able to make all grace abound in you, so that having all sufficiency in all things at all times, you may abound in every good work. (2 Corinthians 9:8)

I want to give you three simple steps to help you get started on the path that God has laid out for you.

1. Start where you are.

Always remember where you are now is not where you have to finish. That choice is yours—*that's on you.* Zechariah 4:10 reads, *"Do not despise these small beginnings, for the Lord rejoices to see the work begin..."* Small beginnings are a good place for God to help you build from!

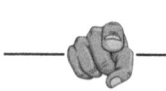

ONE STEP IN GOD'S DIRECTION IS BETTER THAN ONE-HUNDRED STEPS ON YOUR OWN.

The good thing about God is that if we have the courage to step in His direction, He guides our steps. Proverbs 20:24 tells us that *"The Lord directs our steps...."* I can tell you from experience that one step in Gods' direction is better than one-hundred steps on your own. Start where you are and take just one step in God's direction. Eventually, you will find that one step leads to two, then three, and so on.

2. Start with what you have.

This immediately makes me think of the Bible account of what Jesus did with just five loaves and two fish. This truly amazing miracle shows us what God does when you don't feel you have enough.

> *Sometime after this, Jesus crossed to the far shore of the Sea of Galilee (that is, the Sea of Tiberias), and a great crowd of people followed him because they saw the signs he had performed by healing the sick. Then Jesus went up on a mountainside and sat down with his disciples. The Jewish Passover Festival was near.*

> *When Jesus looked up and saw a great crowd coming toward him, he said to Philip, "Where shall we buy bread for these people to eat?" He asked this only to test him, for he already had in mind what he was going to do. Philip answered him, "It would take more than half a year's wages to buy enough bread for each one to have a bite!"*

> *Another of his disciples, Andrew, Simon Peter's brother, spoke up, "Here is a boy with five small barley loaves and two small fish, but how far will they go among so many?"*

> *Jesus said, "Have the people sit down." There was plenty of grass in that place, and they sat down (about five thousand men were there). Jesus then took the loaves, gave thanks, and distributed to those who were seated as much as they wanted. He did the same with the fish.*

> *When they had all had enough to eat, he said to his disciples, "Gather the pieces that are left over. Let nothing be wasted." So, they gathered them and filled twelve baskets with the*

pieces of the five barley loaves left over by those who had eaten. (John 6:1-12)

If you notice, the disciples immediately began to focus on the circumstances, rather than focus on what Jesus could do. I believe we still do this today, and it keeps us from doing great things for God. As soon as difficulties come, we begin to focus on what we're up against, rather than go to God for wisdom for what to do about it.

I always find it a bit amusing that the first thing Jesus said to His disciples in this instance was, "Have the people sit down." Some of us may have said, "Hurry, get to the store, and somebody heat the oven up!" That's not what Jesus said, He simply says, "Have the people sit down."

"LITTLE IS MUCH WHEN GOD IS IN IT!"

Maybe the disciples were thinking that Jesus wants everyone to sit down so He can explain the situation of not having enough food to go around for everyone. Turns out that just the opposite happens. Not only did they have enough to go around for everyone to eat, but Jesus told them to gather the leftovers. Can somebody say, "Little is much when God is in it!" Always remember that you will often have circumstances and challenges that come when you are trying to do something for God, but He's the God of more than enough!

3. Start Now!

It's never too late to do something great for God. The great commission of the New Testament does not age-discriminate. No matter how old (or young) you may be, spiritually speaking, age is just a number. Moses led the Israelites across the Red Sea when he was eighty years old. On the contrary, David defeated Goliath when he was just a teenage boy.

Therefore, go and make disciples of all nations, baptizing them in the name of the Father and of the Son and of the Holy Spirit, and teaching them to obey everything I have commanded you. (Matthew 28:19-20)

Start now and don't stop!

Don't let the regrets of the past stop you.

Don't let the lies of the enemy stop you.

Don't let what others think about you stop you.

Don't let depression and anxiety stop you.

Don't let lack of knowledge stop you.

Don't let lack of resources stop you.

Supplying you with more than enough—*THAT'S ON HIM!* Deciding to just start—*THAT'S ON YOU!*

Applying This Principle–That's on You!

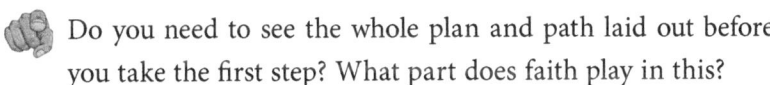 Do you need to see the whole plan and path laid out before you take the first step? What part does faith play in this?

 Read Hebrews 11 and Romans 4. Honestly assess whether you're walking by faith.

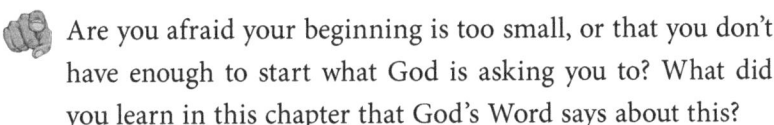 Are you afraid your beginning is too small, or that you don't have enough to start what God is asking you to? What did you learn in this chapter that God's Word says about this?

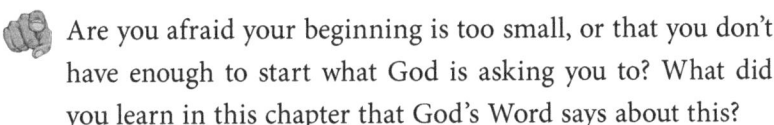 Renew your mind with His Word so you can be bold and courageous, resulting in good success wherever you step forward. Read what the Lord said to Joshua regarding this: Joshua 1:5-9.

Are you afraid you're too young or too old to step out? Read 1 Samuel 17:12-51; 2 Kings 22:1-2; 1 Timothy 4:12; Joshua 14:6-16; Psalm 92:13-15; Psalm 71:18.

Is age a determining factor in God's Kingdom?

 Are you wrongfully disqualifying yourself from starting your God-adventure? Have you identified anything which prevents you from moving into what He's called you to?

 Ask Him to help you overcome fear, wrongful thinking, the fear of others' opinions, lack of resources, age, or any other issue by which you've allowed yourself to be disqualified. He will qualify and enable you for what He's called you too. He is *with you* and *for you* and will *always* lead you in triumph!

God always makes his grace visible in Christ, who includes us as partners of his endless triumph. Through our yielded lives he spreads the fragrance of the knowledge of God everywhere we go. (2 Corinthians 2:14)

FINAL WORDS

My prayer is that you have been encouraged to activate the power of God in your life while reading through the pages of this book. His power is the most unstoppable force humanity will ever encounter. It's the power that saves you and the power that sustains you. The power of God is so great that not even death itself could stop it. It can be hard to comprehend that a born-again believer has this same grave-shattering power living within them!

> *The Spirit of God, who raised Jesus from the dead, lives in you. And just as God raised Christ Jesus from the dead, he will give life to your mortal bodies by this same Spirit living within you. (Romans 8:11)*

I still remember God speaking the simple phrase, "THAT'S ON YOU" into my spirit many years ago. Since then, my life has dramatically changed. Many seasons of life have come and gone. God first spoke this to me when I was a single young man, in search for peace and happiness, and praying that He would make all my dreams come true. I've since been married for nearly 30 years, raised three kids, become a grandpa, and when I look in the mirror, I have gray in my beard. For me, these are all dreams come true, except for the part about the gray in my beard. I keep telling myself that the gray makes me look wise and distinguished. That's the power of positive thinking, right? Well, anyway…

I have been preaching the message "That's on You" all these years. I've heard that the message can be a bit harsh. I even debated whether to have the big finger pointing at you on the cover of this book. To that I say, "It is what it is." If the shoe fits, wear it. Said another way, if that finger points to an area of your heart in conviction, yield to God's

Spirit. Follow His principles so that His great power will be unhindered in you. Nothing in this world could be worth standing in the way of His plan for creating you and the power He's made available to those who follow Him wholeheartedly.

For the eyes of the LORD move to and fro throughout the earth so that He may support those whose heart is completely His. (2 Chronicles 16:9 AMP)

My prayer is that you have now been challenged with this simple phrase, as I was. I pray that you think of the people in your life that need to hear it as well. I pray you have the courage to subtly challenge them with the message of "That's on You."

Notice, I used the word "subtly." How you deliver this message to others makes a difference. I've gotten better at it over the years. You may be surprised at who will respond to it in a positive way. They may be in a season of defeat, like I was, and this simple phrase, paired with some encouragement and prayer, may change their life forever.

If you put this book down and never apply its principles, well, "That's on you." God will not force Himself on you. That's not in His nature. On the other hand, maybe today is the day you dig your heels in and tell the devil and your old man, "That's enough!" Make it a declaration. A declaration is a formal announcement. The word is used in the Bible around 150 times. Yes, I want you to make a formal announcement and say, "That's enough!"

Start today and invite God to write the rest of your story. Trust me, His story for you is better and greater than you could ever imagine.

Now to Him who is able to [carry out His purpose and] do superabundantly more than all that we dare ask or think [infinitely beyond our greatest prayers, hopes, or dreams], according to His power that is at work within us, to Him be the glory in the church and in Christ Jesus throughout all generations forever and ever. Amen. (Ephesians 3:20-21 AMP)

In closing, I'll leave you with a verse of scripture we speak in blessing over our congregation every Sunday at Foundation as we dismiss:

> The LORD BLESS YOU and keep you; the LORD MAKE HIS FACE SHINE ON YOU and be gracious to you; the LORD TURN HIS FACE TOWARD YOU and give you peace. (Numbers 6:24-26)